DATE DUE

Lingering Fever

The author in 1945

Lingering Fever

A World War II
Nurse's Memoir

by LaVonne Telshaw Camp

with a foreword by Connie L. Slewitzke
Brigadier General, U.S. Army, Retired

McFarland & Company, Inc., Publishers
Jefferson, North Carolina, and London

British Library Cataloguing-in-Publication data are available

Library of Congress Cataloguing-in-Publication Data

Camp, LaVonne Telshaw.
    Lingering fever : a World War II nurse's memoir / by LaVonne
Telshaw Camp ; with a foreword by Connie L. Slewitzke.
       p.   cm.
    Includes index.
    ISBN 0-7864-0322-5 (library binding : 50# alkaline paper) ∞
    1. Camp, LaVonne Telshaw.   2. World War, 1939–1945—
Medical care— United States.   3. World War, 1939–1945—Personal
narratives,   American.   4. United States. Army Nurse Corps—
Biography.   5. Nurses—United States—Biography.   I. Title.
D807.U6C36   1997
940.54'7573—dc21   96-48855
                                                   CIP

*No part of this book, specifically including the index, may be reproduced or
transmitted in any form or by any means, electronic or mechanical, including
photocopying or recording, or by any information storage and retrieval system,
without permission in writing from the publisher.*

Manufactured in the United States of America

*McFarland & Company, Inc., Publishers
  Box 611, Jefferson, North Carolina 28640*

To Art

Contents

Foreword by Connie L. Slewitzke,
    Brigadier General, U.S. Army, Retired   1

Introduction   5

1   AT WAR IN THE FAR EAST   7

2   OUR ASSAM DRAGON HOME   11

3   A DATE WITH RED   18

4   WHERE IT ALL STARTED   25

5   ACROSS THE BLUE PACIFIC   32

6   THE 14TH EVACUATION HOSPITAL   39

7   NIGHT DUTY ON THE WARD   50

8   HORSEBACK RIDING IN THE JUNGLE   54

9   A VISIT WITH RED   58

10   A TRIP TO CALCUTTA   71

11   SHOPPING FOR BOOTS WITH A BRITISH COLONEL   79

12   OVER THE HUMP TO CHINA   89

13   A VISIT FROM A JUNGLE BEAST   105

14   A SURREPTITIOUS FLIGHT TO HSIAN, CHINA   113

15   MALAISE AT THE 20TH GENERAL HOSPITAL IN
     LEDO   120

16   A REGULAR ARMY NURSE AT THE 142ND
     GENERAL HOSPITAL   130

Contents

17 LIFE IN CALCUTTA   137

18 RED STOPS BY   143

19 A NEW YEAR'S EVE ESCAPADE   152

20 LEFT BEHIND IN INDIA   157

21 GOING HOME   163

    Epilogue   169

    Index   175

Foreword

by Connie L. Slewitzke

Brigadier General, U.S. Army, Retired

MORE THAN 57,000 Army nurses served in all theaters in World War II. They staffed all types of hospitals, hospital trains, planes, and clearing stations. They were on beachheads in North Africa, Anzio and Normandy. Over 200 died and 1600 nurses were decorated for heroism and bravery under fire. Ms. Camp's memoirs describe her experience as an Army nurse in the China-Burma-India theater (CBI). The nurses found the CBI to have an unforgiving hot and humid climate and environmental conditions not conducive to good health. The isolation was profound. It was an experience that lingered in the psyche for life. Intense physical, mental and professional challenges awaited the young army nurse in the CBI. *Lingering Fever* gives us one nurse's view of her wartime experience.

The China-Burma-India theater was the forgotten theater of World War II. Its importance in keeping the allied supply lines open to Chiang Kai-shek's army was critical to Allied strategy in the Pacific. Once the Japanese captured Rangoon and cut off the Burma Road, the only option open to resupply Chiang's army was by air until a new road was built. The Air Transport Command and Troop Carrier (ATC) pilots risked their lives on every trip over the "Hump," a range of towering mountain peaks with dangerous turbulence.

The CBI's mountainous terrain, impenetrable jungles, hot climate and heavy monsoon rains provided a formidable challenge to military units. The medical challenge was to keep the troops healthy, given the many tropical diseases that most physicians and nurses had only read about in school. That medical admissions surpassed surgical admissions was due to the tactical situation and environmental conditions that predisposed the troops to disease despite strong preventive medicine.

The majority of troops in theater were Chinese, with lesser numbers of Allied forces. The Japanese troops were seasoned, belligerent and very determined in their goal to conquer Asia.

The first U.S. army hospitals arrived in theater in 1942. Then, Army nurses arrived to staff the hospitals. Some were assigned to hospital units in major cities in India, others to Burma and limited numbers to China. Ms. Camp and other nurses were assigned to Burma as replacements for nurses rotating home. Nurses assigned to Burma lived under very primitive conditions. Most had little or no idea of the harsh living and climatic conditions or professional challenges that awaited them. They lived in tents or *bashas*, bamboo huts with little or no protection against wild or domesticated animals, reptiles and mosquitoes. In addition, the cultural and professional adjustments required great mental and physical stamina. However, most nurses were resilient and made the most of this experience. Many of them were young, new to the military with limited orientation to combat nursing and new to the profession of nursing. Most had never traveled out of the United States. They had joined the Army Nurse Corps to serve their country and envisioned that they would be caring for wounded soldiers. In contrast to their expectations, they found that most of their patients were Chinese and medical. Medical nursing does not have the same glamour as trauma nursing although it often requires as much or more nursing time. Caring for the Chinese patients presented professional and communication challenges. It required teaching the young Chinese soldier and basic principles of hygiene and self-care through an interpreter and nonverbal communication that required constant reinforcement. The patients paid little or no attention to doctors' or nurses' orders. They could exhaust the patience of the most dedicated nurses, and yet their good humor could not be ignored.

The long assignment in theater (average two years) affected the physical and mental health of the staff. There were several causes for the morale problems that surfaced: nutrition was deficient as fresh fruits, vegetables and meats were scarce and the cooks developed innovative ways to serve the same food daily; the PX did not carry sufficient supplies for female officers; the rules and regulations discriminated against nurses; nurses were not allowed to fly in theater, forcing them to take a slow and filthy train on rest and recuperation leaves; nurses were not allowed to marry; promotions were slow; uniforms wore out and were difficult to replace; and some units did not have the strong leadership that the situation required. To relieve some of the tension and to raise morale, social and recreational activities were organized and pursued as far as was feasible in a war zone. Romances and friendships formed between the nurses and military men stationed nearby. Ms. Camp has woven accounts of her romance with poignant episodes of her duties as a professional nurse. She took some unauthorized flights with her pilot friend to China and Calcutta, giving little thought to the repercussions that would have followed had something happened. This friendship culminated in marriage after the war.

One can draw direct parallels and differences between Army nursing in the CBI and Vietnam. Nurses' quarters in Vietnam were good compared to the *bashas* in Burma. Hospitals in Vietnam were, however, more vulnerable to enemy attack than those in Burma. In Vietnam, there were no battle lines. Nurses in both areas were young, new to the military, recent graduates, away from home for the first time, in a foreign land, in a combat zone. Medical supplies and treatment in Vietnam were more sophisticated, but staff in both places had to improvise to meet patient needs. The CBI was not the number one priority in the supply channels. Nurses returning from both wars to civilian life had to make adjustments to civilian nursing after the greater responsibilities they had assumed in providing nursing care under combat conditions.

Though Ms. Camp says her book is a love story, it is much more. Her story lingered in her memory and manuscript form for many years. In sharing with the reader her account of wartime service she honors all the heroic and dedicated army nurses who served in World War II. All gave selflessly of themselves so that the nursing care they provided could be of the highest standard possible. They returned home more independent and mature, and with a lifetime of memories and experiences that most would not have again. They were proud to serve and proud of their contributions. The Army Nurse Corps has proudly preserved this heritage of service since its establishment in 1901.

Introduction

THIS IS A MEMOIR of my service as an Army nurse in the China-Burma-India theater during World War II. It is a story of nursing sick and wounded soldiers in the heat, muck, and mud of the jungle, of dealing with loneliness and isolation, of trying to work effectively in an organization where morale had hit rock bottom. For me, a young woman, teetering on the edge of adulthood, it was an overwhelming experience to be catapulted into a world of physical misery, into a hospital unit that had lost its will to perform. I knew little about the diseases I encountered and even less about the Asian soldiers who suffered from them. Nothing in my nursing education had taught me how to deal with rats, men who spit on the floor, soldiers who used firearms to chase gigantic cockroaches, or patients who sold rather than swallowed their medication.

The impact of these wretched conditions was made tolerable by an ongoing romance with one of the airmen who supplied OSS troops, ferried military units around the theater, and flew cargo over the treacherous mountains that separate India from China. With the flimsiest of authorization, I went with him on several of his missions.

The story reveals my uneasiness with my rural background, my timorous attitude toward the opposite sex, and my general social awkwardness. There are touches of humor in this extraordinary experience.

Writing this book was like resuscitating a long-gone experience, breathing life into something that happened almost half a century ago. After arduous hours of trying to get in touch with the person that I once was, visualizing those things that I had written in letters to my parents, and pushing aside the demands of the present, this whole experience began to beat in rhythm with my heart. I began to live it all over again.

Recognizing how hazardous it would be to wholly depend upon memory and its frailty, I read everything I could find about the China-Burma-India theater of war and became aware that the great number of books written about World War II are biased toward the other theaters: Europe, North Africa, and the Pacific. The late Barbara W. Tuchman's book *Stilwell and the American Experience in China*, an official army history by Charles Romanus and Riley Sunderland, and an unpublished document by James H. Stone entitled "US Army Medical Service in Combat in India and Burma, 1942–1945" supplied me with some of the basic information I needed.

I am grateful to Richard Nemiroff, M.D., and his wife, Barbara, who were the first to read my manuscript and who encouraged me to go on with the work. Clara Ruvolo, a columnist for *New Jersey Woman*, who herself was once a nurse, gave me faith in myself when my spirits flagged, as did Fran Sauers, a retired instructor of English at Rutgers University, who edited the original manuscript.

Men and women who appear in this book are very real people, and many of them may recognize themselves in the pages of this volume, but for some I have used fictitious names to protect their privacy and in some instances their reputations. Some of their memories may not be the same as mine, and I did not want to cause discomfort for anyone who was unfortunate enough to be there in the first place.

It all happened long ago and far away, but it is a poignant story of how one young life was forever changed by that enormous upheaval that altered the world.

LAVONNE TELSHAW CAMP
September 1996

Chapter 1

At War in the Far East

I T WAS LATE AFTERNOON. June 1945. Suffocating heat and soaking humidity hung oppressively over the thatched roofs of the buildings in the hospital compound. Except for the chattering of monkeys in the encircling jungle, there was only that peculiar silence born of inertia. A monsoon downpour had washed the area clean of dust, and water rushed in the deep drainage ditches that ran alongside the winding footpaths. The lowering sun was sucking up the moisture in puffs of mist that rose as high as the tallest trees. The heat had wilted my spirits, and a consuming hunger for home lay like lead in my young heart, when my ears caught the unmistakable drone of an approaching C-47. I stepped out of my *basha* and looked up as the plane came in over the tree tops, the prop-wash agitating the leaves and branches of the towering bamboos. The word "Kismet" painted on the nose of the fuselage identified it as the aircraft I had hoped for; the red-headed pilot, waving from the open side window of the cockpit, was the "fly boy" I had been waiting for. He circled, waggled his wings, pulled up and away from the small opening in the dense Assam forest and headed for the air base in Ledo.

He had seen me return his wave as I stood in the narrow path outside my little straw house. It was a signal that I understood the message of his plane's dipping wings and low swoop over the compound, that by nightfall he would arrive at the hospital and together we would return to the air base and spend the evening at the Officers' Club. I was stationed at the nineteen mile mark of the narrow, twisting road; his base was at the initial point of this highway that snaked from Ledo, through Burma, to a junction with the old Burma Road into China. We called it the Ledo Road but it had once been called "Pick's Pike" for General Lewis A. Pick who engineered the road, and before the end of the war would be named "The Stilwell Road" for General Joseph W. Stilwell, commanding general of the theater.

When Kismet appeared in that piece of sky over the cluster of *bashas* that was the 14th Evacuation Hospital, I was both relieved and excited—relieved to know that his mission was completed for that day and he was safe; excited to know that I would see him that night. Just the thought of briefly escaping the enervating malaise that had overtaken me, lifted my spirits up and out of the reality of this place of dankness and rot.

We had come to India at different times and by different routes to serve our country in its military action in Asia during World War II. The passage of time and the chroniclers of history have shed a clearer light on our involvement in the war that was fought against the Japanese. Even though we were eye witnesses to events, we had a very limited understanding of them. Our youthful enthusiasm was focused on the eventual defeat of the Japanese army that had invaded the Asian mainland as well as the many islands in the Pacific, but history has revealed that the war in the China-Burma-India theater was a more tangled campaign than that. The British needed help in keeping the Japanese from breaking through into India; the Chinese needed our war matériel; and the Ledo Road had to be built as a conduit for supplies for the armies of Generalissimo Chiang Kai-shek. A giant airlift over the most treacherous mountains in the world was a major part of the action, as was dropping supplies to the Office of Strategic Services (OSS) troops that were carrying on a guerrilla war in Burma. Hospitals where doctors and nurses could serve the fallen soldiers were also a necessary part of this complex operation.

The people at home were looking in the other direction, toward Europe, where they cheered the victories and shuddered at any setback suffered by allied troops. Except for the battles to secure islands in the Pacific Ocean, few people took an intense interest in what the Japanese were doing on the Asian continent. Many Americans did not even know that a war was being fought in these far off places, nor were they mindful of our specific role in that operation. The CBI was often referred to as the "forgotten campaign." Those of us who were there, however, will never forget. It was a war that involved enemies we had not dreamed of, climate that wrested our energy and vitality, diseases that the western world rarely heard of or had ways to treat, loneliness that sapped our spirits, and encounters with other cultures that were completely foreign to anything we had known.

Nearly a half century has elapsed since the war ended and thousands of us returned to pick up the threads of our lives. For a long time, we did not look back. There was too much to do: educations to pursue, families to be established, homes to build, careers to create. In the vigorous years that followed World War II, America was growing, confident of its virtue and power, flexing its economic muscles, helping other countries to regain their health, and all the while knowing that victory had clothed it in dazzling glory.

Recently I picked up a bundle of faded, mildewed letters, most of them mailed to my parents. They were from Army Post Office, A.P.O., addresses, had no stamps, and bore dates in 1944 and 1945. One of them read:

> As I sit here writing to you, I can hear the Chinese singing their tinkling little chants. In the other direction, down by the river, the Hindus are building a fire to cook their rice. They are singing too, but their music sounds like a wail, not as happy sounding as the Chinese songs.
>
> I miss you all, terribly. The war will be over soon and all of us will be very happy to return to blessed America.
>
> Last night I had a date with a red head. He's one of the pilots who flies cargo over the mountains to China. He's a nice chap—looks like Hot Shot Charlie.

As I continued to read the letters, memories flooded, and I was filled with a great surge of emotion, nostalgia, and the pain of lost youth. I reached far into the past, into the tenderness of girlhood, dredging up moments that had long lay lifeless. World War II belonged to my generation; its impact on my life was greater than any other national upheaval. Young men and women like myself, living in a nation that was just emerging from the Great Depression, were only beginning to venture away from the familiar into the unknown, but none of us contemplated the giant step war demanded. Time has eroded some of my memories of that wartime period, when I served proudly in the Army Nurse Corps, but the fogginess that builds around recollections has never obliterated that extraordinary experience. That air-to-ground contact, for instance, is as vivid today as it was when I was smitten by the boyish pilot who pushed his cap to the back of his head like "Hot Shot Charlie" in the comic strip "Terry and the Pirates." As I breathe life into the past, I scarcely recognize the buoyant young girl and the dauntless young man that occupy the center stage of my memory of that unusual Asian adventure.

Chapter 2

Our Assam Dragon Home

OVER THE DOOR of my *basha* was a slab of wood painted with bold letters, "OUR ASSAM DRAGON HOME." Mine too, I thought. I wondered how I could have been so unlucky as to be sent to this miserable place. Why not England? Or France? Or Hawaii? Or somewhere where people lived in houses and hospitals were not made with thatched roofs and mud floors. I thought about the nurses that we had come to replace, how worn out they looked, how spent and listless. The two women who had lived here before us were the ones who had put the sign over the burlap, hung like a curtain, making it possible to enter or exit as silently as the moonlight came in, in the velvet Indian night. The entrance was low, so I stooped to get back inside and primp a little in anticipation of seeing the pilot who was coming to take me out that night, down the wildly curving Ledo Road to his club, where they had an orchestra made up of men from the base. The music, the air crews and their dates, nurses and Red Cross girls from the 20th General Hospital in Ledo, all helped to create an atmosphere designed to make us forget, if only for a few hours, the loneliness and discomforts that we faced every day.

On the day we had arrived, months before, we had been unceremoniously dumped out of the weapons carrier that had brought us from the Air Transport Command (ATC) Headquarters in Chabua where we had flown from Calcutta. There we had deplaned in a drenching monsoon rain and waited for ground transportation to take us to our assigned hospitals. I had opened a can of C-rations, perhaps seeking a kind of comfort to assuage the bewilderment that was overtaking me. Usually the air was filled with chatter and chuckling when a group of military nurses were gathered in circumstances not related to their pressing responsibilities, but there was an awkward silence among us as we contemplated what lay ahead. I squatted at the edge of the huddled group and ate the scrambled egg and bacon concoction from the little olive drab tin. A single truck drove through the puddles of water accumulated on the field and the driver asked our captain where we were going. Some of the nurses were going to the General Hospital in Ledo, some to the evacuation hospital on the Ledo Road, and a few to the field hospital in Shingbwiyang in Burma. The driver and another soldier put our foot lockers aboard and we followed, carrying our musette bags on our backs and small suitcases that were light enough to be manageable.

That was one of the most depressing rides I had ever had. It may have been interesting, even exciting, had it not rained every inch of the way. After leaving the airbase in Chabua, the road passed through an Assamese village called Tinsukia, where the Americans had a supply depot for petroleum products, a vital ingredient of warfare. Surrounding the little town, were acres and acres of growing tea, the dark green leaves glistening in the falling rain. Then came Ledo, remote and isolated, where the ascending road became a convoluted avenue of slime; the rear end of the truck fish-tailed at every turn and the C-ration that I had eaten hours before sloshed sourly in my stomach. A wave of nausea passed over me, then another, until I finally hung my head over the tailgate and let it go. This was worse than the motion sickness I'd had on the ship crossing the Pacific. At the foot of an incline, there was a single slab of wood with "14th Evac" painted on it. The driver veered off onto a spur of road, into a compound of thatched roof buildings and turned off the motor. Splattered with mud, soaked to the skin, dismayed by the sight of the little hole in the jungle that would be our habitation for as far as we could see into the future, we tried to be jolly and hang onto that special camaraderie that had carried us over rough spots in the past. We dared not reveal, even to each other, that the scene that lay before our eyes had subdued our enthusiasm and increased our misgivings. We gathered in a long barracks with a straw roof, cots lined against the bamboo walls, and an inescapable odor of mildew.

"Officers, welcome to the Waldorf Astoria." The chief nurse of the hospital greeted us with warmth and humor, but I thought there was a touch of pity in her voice. She was glad to see replacements for her staff but she knew that we would never understand what it was like

Nurses lived in these little straw houses called *bashas*. Ours was named "Our Assam Dragon Home."

to work in a place like this until we actually began our duties. She admonished us to behave in a manner commensurate with our professional stature and not to whine or complain because it would do no good.

"We are very glad that you have come. Many of our nurses have been here for a long time, they are tired, they are worn out, and you girls are their ticket to the States," she added. I discerned that just beneath the weariness in her voice there were tears of relief that her own tour of duty was ending. "I will ask you to stay here, in this old officers' ward, until the other nurses get their orders to leave, then you and your chief nurse, Captain Williams, can move into the *bashas* in the nurses' quarters. I'm going home too." The absence of enthusiasm in her greeting portended a lousy assignment. I could tell that she was about at the end of her rope. It didn't take me long to find out why she and the entire organization were suffering from a spiritless languor.

By this time, we had almost forgotten the initial shock of being plunked down in this murky environment and had settled in to become effective members of the hospital's nursing staff. Words that we had never heard were becoming a part of our everyday vocabulary. Until

Corbi, our Burmese bearer, who carried an umbrella to signify his opulence.

that first day, I had never heard the word *basha*, but here I was, standing in one of those thatched roof buildings that I shared with another nurse, Mitzi. Our *basha* had two bedrooms and a common living room, though giving them those familiar names didn't automatically give them an agreeable ambience. We each had a cot overhung with a voluminous mosquito netting and there were a few wide shelves against the wall where we kept our uniforms and other clothing. The living room had some shabby bamboo furniture and a single light bulb that hung forlornly from the ridge pole of the structure. No matter how well thatched the roof, the monsoon rains found ways of seeping through, leaving little puddles on the floor and dampening our bedding and clothing.

Not only did we inherit this *basha* from the nurses who had lived here before us, but we also became the employer of a servant, a young Burmese boy named Corbi who had been their bearer. Corbi kept our *basha* neat and organized, carried our laundry to the *dhobi*, the Indian washerman, polished our leather shoes and carried messages from one *basha* to the other. He arrived at our little home in Assam every morning before seven, carrying with him an umbrella, which, I was told, signified his opulence. He spoke only a few phrases of English, but he seemed to understand everything we said to him. Attending to our needs was a very serious business for this twelve year-old-boy who had a way of anticipating *mem-sahib*'s bidding. We paid him thirty rupees a month. At that time, a rupee was worth about one third of an American dollar, so Corbi's salary was a little over nine dollars a month. We would have been willing to pay him more, but the British had established stringent rules as to how Americans were expected to remunerate local citizens whom they hired. It was not in the best interests of the British to raise the standard of living of Indians or Burmese as it would only create more inflation in an already disturbed economy.

The frame of the building where we had now taken up residence, was made of sturdy bamboo poles. Split bamboo, woven into panels formed the outside walls and the dividing wall between our sleeping quarters. The inside walls were made of Hessian cloth, a rugged burlap type fabric, nailed to the frame to give the whole edifice the appearance of a lined basket. The space between the outer and the inner walls was a runway for the most arrogant, repulsive, and noisome rats imaginable. The awful fact was, Mitzi and I shared our *basha* with numberless big black rodents whose constant scurrying up and down the framing poles was just one more unnerving factor of our existence in this remote corner of the world.

Sometimes it was extremely hot. Nothing stirred. Even the rats would go underground where it might be a little cooler. One wondered what it would feel like to be dry. The humidity was so pervasive that even my cot felt wet. Mold grew in the seams of my shoes overnight. Everything smelled sour, musty, decomposed.

Paths bordered with deep ditches for monsoon downpours were laced throughout the hospital compound.

"At least," I thought, "when the summer monsoons are over, it will be a lot more comfortable up here in the hills than down in Calcutta." It wasn't easy to look neat and well groomed, like I wished I could, but everyone else was in the same boat, which made the situation more tolerable. The dampness made my hair very curly, but some of the nurses' hair-dos were like limp seaweed and there wasn't much they could do about it. All of us were taking on that jaundiced color that resulted from our daily atabrine tablets. Atabrine was used throughout the CBI and Pacific Islands theaters as a prophylactic to protect us from malaria. Neglecting to take your daily dose was a court martial offense. That fresh, healthy look of early youth was beginning to fade; we began to look sallow and fatigued.

The shower was a short distance from the *basha*. In between was the latrine, a two-holer that reminded me of the one on my grandmother's farm back in Pennsylvania. During daylight hours we could use the latrine with a certain degree of privacy; after dark we had to be accompanied by a guard. He waited outside, then walked back to the nurses' quarters with whomever he "guarded." At first, I was over-come with embarrassment at having to be escorted to the toilet by a soldier; it was downright humiliating. But, like many other peculiar practices, it soon became an accepted routine. The commanding officer was adamant in providing a safe environment for his hospital staff, safe from wild animals and marauding natives, but we, the nurses, felt that the "wolves" in the medical corps were the most dangerous people in the compound. One night one of the nurses decided to go to the latrine alone, which most of us tried to do most of the time. When she stepped into the john, the light from her flashlight fell upon a huge coil on the floor. It began unwinding itself and slithering off into the jungle when she screamed for the guard. Snakes and wild beasts were commonly seen in the hospital area and all up and down the Ledo Road. After all, it was we who had invaded their domain, not the other way around.

Chapter 3

A Date with Red

I CAME OUT of the shower—two empty fifty-five gallon fuel drums filled with water that ran out of a two-inch galvanized pipe—feeling just as hot and sticky as I had before going in, but the long afternoon and the rain were ending and things were coming to life as the temperature simmered to a bearable degree. Some of the hospital staff were gathering in the mess tent to eat and curse the food; to share rumors of a war that was slowly grinding down to victory; to exchange their hopes for a new assignment that would whisk them away from this malevolent jungle where they felt so out of touch with the real world. A Lister bag hung gray and flaccid along the path, but I was thirsty and this was the only "safe" water in the compound. Treated with chemicals and hung in the heat, the water that ran from the little faucet that penetrated the gray canvas was brown and turbid. It tasted like mud and chlorine. I drank a few sips of the awful stuff and thought about how good it would be to slake my thirst with water and ice that would be available at the Officers' Club at the air base.

Dressed in bush clothes, long khaki pants, a khaki shirt and high GI shoes, I listened for the rattle of a jeep that was due any time. It would have been fun to dress in a real skirt, or something that would give me that state-side look, but the things we wore were a further protection against malaria. Having seen many soldiers prostrated by this debilitating fever, the agony of their violent shaking chills, their profuse sweats and pounding headaches, I had ample incentive to take my atabrine and cover my body with long sleeves and long trousers. After sundown everyone covered his or her extremities.

Mitzi and I sat in the dusk and chatted while I waited for Red, whose real name was Arthur Camp. It was often the case, in those years, that a man with red hair was called Red, but red-haired girls

Lister bag water was tepid, turbid, and just plain terrible.

seemed to escape that label. I had been introduced to Red by one of our nurses who was having a wild, uninhibited fling with the commanding officer of the airbase. Her feet had hardly touched the ground at the 14th Evac. before she was swept away by this clumsy, womanizing officer, a common occurrence that the more cautious girls soon learned to dodge. There were many philandering men in the military and a few imprudent officers who felt that nurses were sent overseas for their own personal comfort and pleasure, and were indignant when these women let them know otherwise. The ratio of men to women was a bit of good fortune that made even the dowdiest old nurse enjoy a degree of popularity with the guys, a position that she may never have enjoyed before or would ever know again when the war was over. Mitzi and I used to snicker when we saw our chief nurse sashay down the path to her *basha*, with the chief medical officer's arm around her waist.

The author (left) and another nurse dressed in long pants and high shoes for protection from malaria-carrying mosquitoes.

"You can be sure the major wouldn't look at her twice if we were back in the States," Mitzi commented. "Some of these old bags are having the time of their lives out here where there's no competition."

"She might be quite attractive if she didn't have to wear those baggy seersucker clothes and those hightop shoes," I said. "She's a funny old frump, but I'm sure she's very keen on keeping all of us happy. She's been exceptionally agreeable about my work schedule, and she's always ready to come to my rescue when I have a problem. I like the old girl." Mitzi and I were young compared to many of the nurses. They seemed old to us although they were probably in their thirties. Captain Williams was well into her forties—maybe more.

"I can't wait to get down to the airbase and have a cold drink," I said to Mitzi. "There is almost never any ice at our club. The doctors hang out there and guzzle all day—some of them, anyway. I heard that some of our medical officers have been out of the States for over three years, and several of them are not even assigned. They're waiting for orders to get out of here."

"I swear some of them have gone 'round the bend," Mitzi confided. "Not that guy who hangs out around your ward, Tex. He's really agreeable to help when we need a doctor, if we can get him to leave that ward where you're working."

"That's why I don't want to get ice at our club, Mitzi. Tex might be there and when he finds out I'm going with one of the pilots from Ledo, he'll have a fit. He hardly lets me out of his sight."

Red didn't even get out of the jeep when he came. I said "so long" to Mitzi and we headed down the twisting road toward Ledo. I had the feeling that I was escaping from something, running away from suffocation. No matter how bumpy the road, how much the mud splatted over me, I loved that wild ride in the open jeep with Red at the wheel. Sometimes, if the mud had dried, we'd be covered with dust from head to toe.

"Where were you coming from when you flew over my *basha* this afternoon?" I asked.

"I was coming in from Myitkyina. We've been carrying pipe for the pipeline. I think they hope to stretch the line from Myitkyina to Kunming before it's over."

If the construction of the Ledo Road had been one of the most extravagant engineering feats of World War II, the pipeline that paralleled it was equally so. Thousands of tons of pipe were flown to the forward areas by airmen from the United States. Keeping planes and ground vehicles supplied with fuel was essential to the entire military effort. Even the generators that supplied light and energy to our hospital needed fuel. From Calcutta, gasoline came by rail, pipeline, and river barge, but it had to be forwarded from Assam to Burma and on into China. The British and the Chinese could not fight effectively against the Japanese without the fuel that America provided.

Riding to and from the 14th Evac. and the air base in Ledo, I learned about the missions that Red flew. I tried to get a handle on the military progress of the war, mostly because I was so eager to have it over with and go home. It was hard to imagine that anything that happened in this God-forsaken spot could make any difference between defeat and victory for there were no clearly drawn battle lines. Even the troops who were supposedly on our side were not to be trusted. Some Indian units had defected to the Japanese; some Chinese were avoiding the enemy to husband their ammunition for use against their Communist brothers. It seemed a confused tangle of obstructed purposes and questionable loyalties.

"I haven't been here very long, and I've had enough already. There is no escape from the heat, and these monsoon rains keep everything saturated," I complained.

"You'll get used to it. And the weather will improve. I just hope we're all out of here before then," Red said, as he pulled the jeep into an open area near the Officers' Club.

Strains of "Begin the Beguine" could be heard as soon as he killed the motor. It was like therapy, after a tough week on the wards, trying to practice nursing in an environment so foreign to what we had been accustomed. I didn't know anything about the diseases we were treating—couldn't even pronounce the names of most of them: leishmaniasis, shistosomiasis, kala-azar, tsutsugamushi fever, dengue, and most of all, malaria, in its most virulent form. I would, in time, get to know them well, but in the meantime, I was frustrated and disheartened. We walked into the club and Red introduced me to some men from his squadron. A few couples were dancing to the "big band" music. The colored parachutes they had used to decorate the building gave it a bright and lively look and dispelled the grim truth of the soggy, mildewed atmosphere of Ledo.

Officers' Club at Ledo Airbase decorated with colored parachutes used for dropping supplies behind enemy lines.

The music changed my whole outlook on things. It was a layer of back home spread over the heat, dirt, and wretchedness of a land that none of us had ever dreamed about. We may have learned about Assam in our geography classes, but we probably thought about it in the same way we thought about Jupiter or Mars. As the night wore on, the band got better, the men played louder and sweated more, as if their exertion would win the war. "I'm Gonna Buy a Paper Doll" came on the heels of "Pistol Packin' Mama," then everyone joined in singing when they played that bawdy song, "Roll Me Over in the Clover." It seemed as though all the lusty feelings that were stored up in these young men were given expression in the vigorous singing of ribald songs.

After a long time, Red asked me to dance. The orchestra was playing "Darling, Je Vous Aime Beaucoup," a lilting song of love that was very popular all through the war. He put his arm around my waist and we dragged our feet, mine clad in those heavy high-top shoes, across the concrete floor, quite ungracefully. I could tell that he was an inexperienced dancer—not that I was so great myself, but I had enjoyed the dances we had in nursing school. We made an ungainly couple out there clunking around, feeling clumsy and self-conscious.

At the end of a long night of feeling more at home than in Assam, we drove back to the hospital. The moonlight on the road and on the lofty tops of the bamboos was brilliant and beautiful, a shimmering luminescence over a primitive landscape where we, two young Americans, were learning much about the dislocations of war. We were, at the same time, discovering in ourselves new emotions and a new tenuous maturity.

Chapter 4

Where It All Started

WHEN THE WAR began, I was a student nurse at the Moses Taylor Hospital School of Nursing, Scranton, Pennsylvania a small teaching facility deep in the heart of the anthracite coal mining industry. Because some of the nursing disciplines were not available to us in this limited-size institution, we affiliated with the New York Hospital-Cornell University School of Nursing in Manhattan. Through most of the months of my arduous "training," as nursing school was then called, the war drained off doctors and nurses from the civilian hospitals, leaving us with interminable hours of hard work and awesome responsibility. Those were the days when nursing was taught in a hospital setting. The classes conducted on the premises and the nursing procedures were explained and demonstrated, then practiced under the stringent supervision of qualified professionals. This was an effective way of keeping the theory of nursing and the practice of nursing from becoming separated. We developed nursing skills that were truly responsible for bringing sick and broken people back to wellness, and we nurtured in our hearts a pride in excellence as well as the spirit of caring. Nursing, as a profession, has survived the vicissitudes of a health care system in upheaval, and has become the cornerstone of any effectively functioning hospital. Nurses have played a vital role in wars that have been fought since World War II, but that global conflict marked the beginning of a new perception of women in the military, and it changed the character of nursing in a most definitive way.

Graduation came, state board examinations followed, and then a job—the going salary was about one hundred fifty dollars a month. After three and a half years of penury, that sounded like a fortune. My first position was as a staff nurse at the New York Hospital, where I felt quite comfortable since many of my student days had been spent there. However, after a short time, the glamour of being in New York wore thin and I decided to respond to President Roosevelt's plea for nurses to serve in military hospitals. This was one of the first major decisions about my own life that I had ever made without consulting anyone else.

It had been a bright autumn morning, my day off duty, when I took those first steps to actualize my resolution. I dressed in a red plaid skirt, a red sweater, and put on my roller skates. Another nurse and I had just purchased skates so we could enjoy the fun of whipping around Central Park. We needed the feel of the outdoors after hours of confinement to the hospital environment. I skated down Fifth Avenue to a big gray building where a huge American flag and an equally large Red Cross flag were thrust out over the sidewalk, casting shadows on the hurrying pedestrians. On the curb, I exchanged the roller skates for a pair of saddle shoes, walked into the building and asked the receptionist to direct me to the recruiting office.

"May I ask," she glowered at me, "what you are going to do in the recruiting office?"

"I'm going to join the Army Nurse Corps," I answered, almost inaudibly, standing there holding roller skates and looking very young. She may have thought I was no more than an adolescent dreaming of adventure, and she was not far off target, even though I had just passed my twenty-first birthday. When I told her that I was a registered nurse, she looked at me with bare-faced skepticism before she showed me where the recruiting office was. With the appropriate papers signed, I resigned my position at the hospital, packed my books and clothing, went home to say goodbye, then puzzled over why I had made such a decision. It seemed like the natural thing to do, for we had been at war a long time. The war had touched everyone's life in one way or another, and being a nurse gave me the feeling that I could make a meaningful contribution to the war effort.

Basic training at Fort Dix was a nightmare of trudging through the mud, slush, rain, and snow of winter in the New Jersey Pine Barrens. I had exchanged my crisp, white life for a homogeneous environment of olive drab, a color that reminded me of chewed up forest and muddy earth, with a touch of axle grease to assure the drabness.

Everything they taught us in basic training was related to soldiering and very little instruction about procedures in military hospitals.

It was a toughening up process designed to make us physically fit enough to pitch hospital tents, crawl through an infiltration course, survive the lung-searing odor of chlorine gas, and many other gross muscle skills that were once confined to the training of male soldiers. The sergeant who took us into the field for drills, for long marches and for gas-mask procedures, was sadistic. His goal seemed to be to show us that women had no place in this man's army, and he set out to prove it in his own merciless way. We marched for miles with a heavy load of field equipment, mess kits, and a helmet that weighed more than four pounds. Our boots were sometimes sucked deep into soupy mud, making every step a struggle to get one foot ahead of the other. He succeeded in making every one of us as mad as hell, and I learned then, that anger can generate strength and stamina impossible under more serene circumstances. Basic training lasted for only a month, and that was a good thing, for most of us would not have survived those daily drills. I began to feel very fit, gained a few pounds of solid brawn and ate like a horse. The food at Fort Dix was superb, cooked and served by German prisoners of war who leered at us with Teutonic ferocity.

Our government-issue clothing came in two sizes: large and colossal. A pair of olive drab "snuggies" clung to me and felt good in the unheated, frosty barracks, but the crotch hovered around my knees. We all howled with laughter at the sight of female derrières clothed in these ridiculous undergarments. Because the clothing they gave us was so suggestive of winter, I wrote to my parents and told them that I expected to be sent to the Aleutian Islands.

The day before our basic training ended we all decided to celebrate off base. We piled into a local tavern called Baloney Joe's. This was the first time in my life that I had ever been in a bar, or been with people who were accustomed to drinking. Except for rural bums who drank hard cider, and for what I had learned about *delirium tremens* in nursing school, I knew nothing about alcohol. Most of my adolescent years, while going to high school, I had lived in the home of a Presbyterian minister and his family. Liquor was not a part of our lives, but I was not prudish—just unfamiliar with it. Everyone in the bar was drinking something. I wanted a coke but was too chicken to say so, so I ordered a beer and tried to act as though I'd been drinking all my life. The second one was really too much. I remember noise, jostling,

Basic training at Fort Dix. We tried on our seersucker uniforms but never wore them there. (Author far left.)

singing ribald songs, and pledging forever to remember these comrades who would leave for faraway places on the morrow. Had it not been for a letter I had written to my mother, and her having saved all the epistles I mailed home, I would not have remembered Baloney Joe's at all.

The next morning we graduated, become second lieutenants and pinned single gold bars on our epaulets. Half of the class did not feel well enough to attend the ceremony because of vomiting and diarrhea, conveniently attributed to food poisoning. After the rather colorless military ritual, our captain hand-delivered orders to each of us. Everyone was assigned to a military hospital in the mid–Atlantic area, wiping away anyone's dream of going overseas. I was sent to Camp Upton in Patchogue, New York, an isolated spot out on Long Island where an enormous rehabilitation hospital had been set up.

At Upton, I learned what an Army nurse needed to know to efficiently run a ward of men recovering from battle wounds, how to be a leader and manage the enlisted personnel who worked with the patients, and how to cope with the terrible hurt of seeing young men permanently impaired. Underneath the bold front that I turned to the world lay an amorphous mass churning with insecurity and uncertainty.

I had no more than settled in, made some new companions and found that I could take a train back to Manhattan to see my old friends at the New York Hospital when I was sent to a point of embarkation. There were about a dozen nurses who were selected for an overseas assignment, replacements for women who had been out of the country for a long time and were ready to come home. In this group was Mitzi, who would share my life for many months into the future. She was a solid gold girl with the *sang-froid* that I had so little of, and a maturity that I still aspired to attain. Mitzi had grown up in New York; I was the product of rural America. She knew how to tell some guy to get lost; I knew how to get the mud off my shoes. We both knew how to plan and give good nursing care, run a medical or a surgical unit, recognize a patient's need for medical attention, scrub for any kind of surgery, administer medications and treatments prescribed by the physician, and provide the proper documentation that our jobs demanded. Having a buddie like Mitzi was a genuine plus, considering the assignments that befell us.

The patients on the ward where I worked were genuinely upset when they heard that I was going overseas. They begged me not to go. A veteran from the Pacific warned, "If ya wanna get old, Lieutenant, jes go out to the Philippines. They got it all there—dysentery, malaria, crud and rot. Stay home. Stay home an' marry me." Unsettling comments like this were directed my way every day, from soldiers who seemed caring and protective. There was no romance in war as far as they were concerned; it was a hellishly cruel experience that had deflowered their youth and returned them home, scarred and maimed for the rest of their lives.

New York was one of the giant crossroads of the world. Its streets bustled with military men and women, some of them settling in, others just passing through to taste the city's delights. The harbor was awash with shipping and with incoming and outgoing troops to the European theater. War matériel left our shores in an uninterrupted flow to support our European allies and our own overseas armies. Everything was turned out in olive drab. The color itself made a somber statement about the world's condition. It was not business as usual; it was business as battle. Winning was at our fingertips, but it was not yet time to celebrate. Each of us had a job to do, and with that peculiar enthusiasm that belongs to the young, we couldn't wait to get into the fray and show our mettle. In a crush of noise and confusion, we boarded a troop train in Grand Central Station and headed for California.

With every mile that slipped under the train as it rolled over this magnificent nation, I felt a strange aloneness, a stretching of family ties to an imperceptible thinness, my support system receding far into the background as I realized that I was on my own. My eyes scanned the lofty peaks, followed the wandering rivers and streams, warmed at the sight of farms and hamlets, and fought back a tear or two as, for the first time, I experienced the undulating splendor of my own country.

It took four days to get to Camp Beale in northern California, and it wasn't all a matter of absorbing the exquisite scenery. The train was dirty and overheated, not to mention overloaded. The rush to eat in the dining car was reminiscent of feeding time at the hog trough back on the farm. The incessant chatter of women, the boisterous clamor of young men bound for war, the unceasing clatter of wheel on rail, all produced a din that set my nerves on edge. Added to everything was the inability to keep clean. My neck had rings of sooty dirt, my hair was strung out and oily, my clothes were wrinkled and sweaty. I hated it. Why had I opted for this kind of life? Had I know then, that other trains in other places were carrying people to their extinction, that the passengers were cold and without food, that their fragile undernourished bodies would be used to labor for the grisly purposes of the Nazi madmen, I would not have complained. The horrible, tangled mess of World War II would be disclosed later, but in the meantime, although an active participant, I was blind to the enormity of the conflict.

Everyone in the military knew that "hurry up and wait" was a factor of our very existence. We had been rushed to the West Coast only to languish there until transportation became available for moving us forward. When we left Camp Beale we expected the train to take us to a port but it took us deep into the desert east of Los Angeles and south of the San Bernadino National Forest to a place called Anza. I expect it was just a practice maneuver, but every morning we were ordered to have our gear packed and hauled out to the line where roll was called, only to be dismissed and sent back to our barracks. The bitching reached a crescendo. Everyone was exhausted from doing nothing, waiting for something to happen. Then one morning as we approached the mustering area, gear in tow, a military band struck up "As the Caissons Go Rolling Along" and a wild euphoria erupted. We were pumped up with an enthusiasm that washed away the tedium of waiting. We boarded a train for the port of San Pedro where the USS *General H.B. Freeman* waited to take us on its maiden voyage.

Chapter 5

Across the Blue Pacific

THE LONG TRIP across the blue Pacific was, above all else, boring. There were some moments of hilarity when we became "Shellbacks" as we crossed the equator and "Royal Dragons" as we sailed over the international date line, but mostly it was forty-one days of anxiety, wondering where the ship was taking us, the three thousand troops below and the handful of women on the superstructures. There were glorious sunsets at sea that etched their beauty in my memory forever, great swatches of lavender, pink, and gold brushed across the electric blue of the sky, a glimpse of something related to eternity, expressed in a way that made a profound impression on me and my relationship with the planet I lived on.

The nurses on board, as well as some women from the Red Cross who were sailing with us, were not allowed to go on the decks below. Packed three deep in our cramped little stateroom, we were allowed on the deck just under the bridge and other areas of the vessel's superstructure. As we approached the equator, it was miserably hot, but our discomfort was nothing compared to the distress of the men who were crowded into the tiny spaces allotted to them in the hold. They came out on the decks to sleep, for after the sun went down and the heat abated, the air was soft and soothing. One of the nurses aboard wandered about the decks during the night and the rumor that followed gave cause for her to be known evermore as "horizontal Harriet."

"What do you think prompted what's-her-name to wander the decks while all those GIs were sleeping?" I asked Mitzi.

"Oh, I knew her back at Upton. She's just got hot pants and she doesn't use her head. I'm surprised she was picked for overseas service," Mitzi said. "The officers back there all knew she had round heels. They

Settling into our stateroom on the USS *General H. B. Freeman*. It took 41 days to reach our destination. (Author standing.)

made fun of her. I still can't figure out why they considered her for foreign duty."

"She acts a little desperate to me. I'll bet she's afraid and she's acting rash to cover up her anxiety. She might be a section eight. I've heard about lots of service people who were really psycho and acted out in outrageous ways." It seemed kinder to me to think of Harriet as being emotionally disturbed.

"It's jerks like her who give all us nurses a bad reputation. Those men down on the decks think of nurses as real helpers, solid friends they can lean on if they get shot-up or if they're sick, and that's what we are, really. Then that nympho rolls around with a few GIs and her behavior rubs off on all of us." Mitzi sounded irate about the affair, so we didn't talk about it further. Nobody talked about it, and everybody avoided Harriet as though she were grossly contaminated.

At some unmarked spot on the high seas, we began a total blackout of the ship. There was still the gruesome possibility that a Japanese

Laundry problems aboard ship. It was difficult to find your own underwear. (Author on left.)

submarine would aim a deadly torpedo at the USS *General H.B. Freeman*, a liberty ship that had not yet picked up the destroyer escort that would take us safely to our destination. There continued to be a lot of speculation as to where we were going, the usual guess being the Philippines, although one of the ship's officers hinted to me that he believed we would put in somewhere in Australia. He ventured to say that after such a long journey, we might even have a few days shore leave, as there would be a need to take on water and provisions. It didn't take much imagination then, to figure out that an extension of a sea trip from Australia could only mean the likelihood of sailing into the Indian Ocean and docking in Calcutta.

As the darkened ship sliced silently through the rise and fall of endless water, tension in the ship's crew became more apparent. One of the portholes in our stateroom was leaking light, so a sailor was sent up to put some insulating material around the opening. He was a tall, handsome, blonde kid from Texas, and every girl in the stateroom, about sixteen of us, fell in love with him on the spot. He didn't tell me this until much later, that every day he came to the stateroom to check the porthole, he actually was pulling out some of the insulation so that the light would leak again and he could return at night to fix it. Our young men, soldiers and sailors, hungered for the company of women, probably because girls reminded them of home and of the life they had left behind and dreamed of returning to.

The equatorial heat was replaced with cold gales and a coating of ice on the rails. We pitched through the rough seas of the Bass Strait between Tasmania and Australia, then across the Great Australian Bight. I lay in my bunk, holding my helmet which was only a few shades darker green than I. The ship with its cargo of troops docked on the western shore of this island continent, in Freemantle, a tiny village, the port of Perth. The captain announced that we would spend three days in port and that shore leave would be granted to the officers and men according to a schedule posted in the ward room. Naturally, we were all elated with the idea of escaping the confinement of the *Freeman* and once again feel the earth under our feet. When the schedule went up, we realized that the captain had pulled off a great *coup* for his ship's officers. On the first day ashore, only female officers were on the list, leaving all the army men, medical officers, and other passengers that we had come to know so well, confined to the ship, but the crew officers could take the girls into town on dates. The howling that went up was but a futile noise, as the captain has the final word on everything related to his command.

When I walked down the gangplank, Johnny, the Texas kid who had rigged the porthole in our stateroom, was waiting for me. We boarded a train, the quaintest little vehicle I'd ever seen, and sat in a compartment that held only four people. Johnny had never been to Australia before, either, so we were just blundering our way along, using our unquestionable status as Americans to invade and investigate. The Aussies loved us. We were surrounded with good wishes, good will, and good beer. We went to a club, a place where young folks, mostly servicemen, gathered to dine, to dance, and to drink. It was loud and campy, but great fun to be with our Australian cousins, listen to their unique dialect and outlandish expressions. A pretty Australian girl asked, while we were in the ladies' room, "Are you knocked up?" Because I didn't know at the time that she meant, "Are you tired?" I was stunned and indignant.

We ate and danced and drank their beer. Suddenly I saw Johnny, flat on the floor. He was totally inebriated but had not exhibited one sign of it prior to his precipitous drop into oblivion. And there, standing over him, was his shipboard buddy, a bandy-legged little weasel of a man, so homely as to be a caricature of Popeye. He explained to me that he had made an earlier arrangement with Johnny, that should something of this nature happen, he would be responsible for getting me back to the ship on time. Johnny had extracted a solemn promise from him to see to his date's well-being. The gangway was flooded with light as we made our way up, under the curious eyes of the officers who had stayed on board. They were all leaning over the rail to see who the nurses had chosen as escorts for the night-on-the-town. Here I was, being brought up the gangway by Johnny's uncomely friend, grinning as though he'd won first prize for best heifer at the county fair. Not only had I broken the code of behavior of an office by fraternizing with an enlisted man, it appeared that I'd chosen the court jester of the USS *General H.B. Freeman*. Whistles, boos, and catcalls were showered on me as I walked the gangplank of embarrassment. My humiliation was complete when I received a reprimand from the captain.

I hated getting back on ship after three days in port. The sense of confinement was smothering and the uncertainty of what Calcutta would be like ate away at the edges of my composure. As if to take my mind off apprehensions, the Indian Ocean displayed some of the most magnificent sunrises and sunsets that I had ever seen. Sometimes great black clouds would rise over the sea and a cleft in their billowing darkness was lighted by a scarf of magenta, the sun settling out of the sky into a watery horizon. Another time the sky would be free of any cloud formation, just a pristine blue that reflected into the ocean where fish leaped from the water, shimmered briefly, then sank into their preflight domain. Frequently there were freshening showers, rain that was much easier to live with than the monsoon downpours that I would soon come to know. The Bay of Bengal brought us to the mouth of the Hooghly River, one of the wide openings that forms the giant delta of the Ganges. The peculiar odor of musty India was already in my nostrils. As far as the eye could see, the water and the land mingled in a green-brown paludel landscape. Huts on stilts sprang out of the silt where stooped figures were working at some primitive agricultural enterprise. As we sailed into the river and toward the docks of Calcutta,

Debarking in Australia. After a month at sea this was a real thrill.

I watched the milling people and the cows and buffaloes that came to the water's edge. Our voyage was over. We had been at sea for forty-one days. The most urgent thing in my mind was where new orders would send me. I had hoped to see what this bewildering metropolis was like, but there was little time for that. Some of the nurses were assigned to the 142nd General Hospital in the city, and some to other general hospitals in the theater, but a few of us were sent to the forward areas to field, evacuation and station hospitals. "Horizontal Harriet" was sent back to the States.

All these events seemed years ago. There were times, in my little thatched house, that I felt I'd been there forever, and all my past life was a dream bereft of reality. There was, however, a peculiar kind of

On the docks in Calcutta. We were all overwhelmed with the smell of India and apprehensive about our assignments.

personal growth in being so displaced. Living in my own American culture, I may have been blind to its character; living at such a distance, I could be objective about our nation and what it meant to be part of it. Whenever my mind was not focused on my work with the sick and wounded, or was absorbed by my romantic infatuation with Red, I thought about home and longed to be there.

Chapter 6

The 14th Evacuation Hospital

MY FIRST ASSIGNMENT at the 14th Evacuation Hospital was to a ward filled with Chinese patients, perhaps fifty men. The Chinese Army provided me with an interpreter, a real necessity, considering the communication problems that I faced. Yang Jei-pen was a serious young man, well educated by oriental standards, and very helpful in keeping the names of the patients sorted out. Unfortunately, he was not there all the time, and the Chinese ward boy who lived in the ward spoke little English. I had a difficult time keeping the Wongs and the Wangs, the Hos and the Hus straight in my mind, which made giving medications and keeping records a nightmare. I quickly learned the Chinese numbering system, numbered each man's straw pallet, called a *chwáng*, and identified the patient by the number on his *chwáng* Alas, they switched *chwángs* whenever they felt like it, and laughed uproariously at their ability to confuse and frustrate me. I found it impossible to keep an accurate census. Sometimes when I came on duty a half dozen patients would be missing, and I later learned that they had returned to their military units without benefit of medical discharge.

Prior to arriving at this isolated hospital, I had not realized what role the Chinese played in the theater's military operation, nor did I know about the urgency that America felt about keeping China involved in the war. Had this enormous country succumbed to the occupation by Japan, the United States could not have fulfilled its mission in Asia. The commanding general of the CBI, General Joseph W. Stilwell, had been responsible for taking these Chinese peasants and turning them into an effective fighting force in the retaking of Burma from the Japanese. In Ramgarh, India, he trained several units of Chinese soldiers, equipped them as well as their American counterparts,

The author and Yang Jei-pen, our Chinese interpreter.

and gave them the humane treatment that they had not known before. Recruits who came to the Chinese Army had been victims of press gangs, forced into military service because they could not buy themselves out of it. Tied together with rope, they were marched to base camp and given three weeks training before being thrown into combat.

Many of them marched in sandals made of straw and rope and slept under a blanket that they shared with four other soldiers. They were malnourished, ravaged with disease and had no spirit of aggressiveness that a soldier needs. Stilwell took these men and their officers and transformed them into a healthy army. He clothed them, fed them, inoculated them against disease where vaccines were available, and hospitalized them in American hospitals when they needed treatment.

Not all Chinese soldiers were fortunate enough to fall under the aegis of Stilwell and the Americans. Some of them were replacements, poorly equipped, poorly nourished and totally untrained. China had been fighting the Japanese since it had been invaded in 1937. They were tired of war, but were beginning to realize that until the Japanese were driven from the mainland of Asia, they would never be free people. Many of the patients at the 14th Evac. were casualties of the campaign to take North Burma. Those wounded in battle were far outnumbered by those who had fallen victim to tropical disease.

Many of the staff at the hospital, men and women who had been associated with the Chinese Army for a long time, were squeezed dry of compassion. They considered these soldiers as "hopeless, unreliable, corrupt, thieving sons-of-bitches" and seemed reluctant to go out of their way to offer treatment. It was nearly impossible for me to get a medical officer to look at a patient. Many of our doctors had been in the Pacific campaign for an extended time and were shipped to the CBI for yet another long tour of duty. Theirs was a malignant apathy toward the Chinese patients, for they saw in these men a callous attitude toward human life, and they felt that their compassion was wasted. This had not been the case earlier in the campaign. There had been a splendid *esprit de corps*, but month upon month of intolerable conditions had wrung the juices of empathy from their very souls.

During World War II, the hospitals that provided medical services to our armed forces were first established as separate institutions in the States. Usually they were formed by a group of volunteers from medical schools and hospitals. The physicians and nurses, as well as technicians and other personnel necessary to the functioning of a hospital, were carefully selected and were particularly well qualified for the highest type of medical work. The *esprit de corps* and the morale of these groups was especially high, as they were identified with the prestigious institutions they represented. They had worked as a team in the civilian world and were enthusiastic about exercising their skills in the combat areas of war, or anywhere our fallen soldiers needed their special expertise. When these units were called to active duty, they were given a period of military training to familiarize them with army routines and procedures, then placed under the command of regular army officers. The 14th Evacuation Hospital was established by the University of Southern California and the 20th General Hospital was initially made up of physicians, nurses, and technicians from the University of Pennsylvania. I did not belong to this kind of group, but was sent overseas as a replacement for a nurse who had been at the 14th Evac. since its inception. She had the distinct advantage of belonging to an assemblage of professionals that had trained and worked together for many months. Her daily life was supported by the fellowship and camaraderie of her peers and their long association with each other. On the other hand, she had been exposed to the horrors of combat injuries, had worked lengthy hours under appalling circumstances and had been in the theater for such a long time that her health was compromised and her vitality depleted. I came without a "life support system," a newly graduated nurse, with very little experience beyond what I had learned as a student, thrown into an organization that was corroding from lack of spirit and breaking down from an exhausted will to perform. Society had insulated me from the "real" world. All my young life had been given over to learning, to getting as much education as I could afford, seeking a place for myself in my chosen profession, which, in those years did not enjoy the almost limitless boundaries that it does today. Thrust into the strange and alien environment of Assam, working with Chinese patients—I had never known a person from China in my entire life—I had to make all kinds of adjustments in every region of my mind, just to survive. It was my intention to do a good job, to exercise my nursing expertise where it was needed, be it for the sick Chinese or for our own military patients, but I began to feel that nobody really gave a damn. There were many men and women like myself in World War II who found themselves unprepared for their roles but they learned quickly and functioned far better than they ever dreamed they could.

The 14th Evac. was built originally for seven hundred fifty patients. During the campaign to recover North Burma from the Japanese, the

Ambulatory Chinese patients at 14th Evac.

14th was asked to establish a branch hospital to receive casualties from the 5307th Provisional Unit (Special) code named GALAHAD, later known as Merrill's Marauders for Col. Frank Merrill, its commanding officer. These three thousand combat troops penetrated deep behind enemy lines, pushed through the putrefying jungle to flank the Japanese. Casualties, disease and fatigue ravaged their ranks. As fast as the planes could evacuate the wounded, they came in and filled the beds. There were no helicopters, just some L-5s with courageous pilots who were willing to risk being picked off by Japanese Zeros while they searched for a clearing where they could land. Many of these patients were seriously and acutely ill, suffering from exhaustion, malnutrition, typhus, malaria and amoebic dysentery. After months of horrendous conditions of jungle warfare, some of the men were more dead than alive by the time they reached the hospital. The two sections of the 14th Evacuation Hospital which were equipped and staffed for seven hundred fifty patients, now had two thousand eight hundred sick or wounded soldiers, American and Chinese, and even some British and Indians. Not all the casualties could be evacuated from this guerrilla action by air; many of them were brought in after days of struggling through thick forests, swollen rivers and streams, and mountainous terrain that required death defying efforts to traverse. Doctors, nurses and enlisted men worked fourteen and eighteen hours a day. After the battle to take Myitkyina, the patient population began to level off, but there was still much work to be done. It was at this time that my group arrived to relieve some of the staff. A great number of the remaining patients were Chinese, full of worms and other parasites, venereal disease, tuberculosis and dysentery. The morale of the hospital unit was on a precipitous decline.

I had the temerity to approach my nursing job in this ward of disease-ridden men as though the outcome of the war depended upon it. We women, fresh from the States, must have looked a little foolish to the veterans who had been there for many months. After a few encounters with the reality of nursing in a thatched hut, of seeing patients sell their medications, of watching rats run under the *chwángs*, I was considerably subdued and had a better appreciation of the attitudes that prevailed.

The long *basha* that housed the patients was similar to all the other buildings in the compound. The floor was packed-down dirt that promptly became mud where the rain fell from leaks in the roof. The patients' *chwángs*, lined up on either wall, were raised a foot or so off the earthen floor. At one end of the building a small room, partitioned off with a woven bamboo wall, was the nurses' station. Here I kept the meager equipment needed: medications, needles and syringes, a few treatment trays, and the patients' medical records. Just outside this room was a basin of Lysol solution on a little table where I could immerse my hands after ministering to an infected patient, dressing a purulent wound, or cleaning up an ulcerated mouth. I chuckled to myself, thinking of the impeccable aseptic technique that I had been taught to use.

The Chinese did not have the basic understanding of personal hygiene, say nothing of ordinary prophylaxis. Several times a day, I had to confiscate the table that held the Lysol solution from the middle of the ward where they had taken it to roll out their noodles, their *myán*. Cooking is a very serious activity among all Chinese. They built little fires in the middle of the ward, the flammability of the straw not withstanding, and cooked anything they could get their hands on. They gathered plants from the jungle, things that they knew were edible, and caught fish in a nearby river. Our mess supplied them with rice, but their cooks were responsible for feeding their own men. Frequently, I was overcome with the odors in the ward. Mixed with foul smells of human waste there was an overpowering aroma of garlic. Under their *chwángs*, I found tins of soil with garlic growing in them.

They always offered me something to eat, and I was always saying, "*Wo méi-you wèi-kou*," which translates, "I have no appetite." One day one of the patients brought me a bowl of rice; on top lay a small fish, staring up at me with its boiled eye. My stomach did a somersault. Those patients who were able to leave their *chwángs* gathered in the center of the ward for their *chá and fàn*, tea and rice, brought to them from an outside kitchen. The cook, with a pole slung over his shoulder, carried the food in old fuel cans that hung from the ends of the pole. No matter where the Chinese army went, there was always one man, ladden with rattling pots and pans, prepared to cook for the men. Every soldier had a blue sock wrapped around his neck, filled with rice to sustain him in the field.

I enjoyed that time of day when the cook brought the tea and rice. Those patients who could ambulate under their own steam would gather, squat on their haunches and wait for their rice bowls to be filled. Their conversation, always punctuated with great bursts of laughter, made me feel good, even though I hadn't the vaguest idea what was bringing such apparent joy. They held the rice bowls up to their chins and with two chop sticks held close together they shoveled the rice into their mouths, down to the very last grain. Afterward they drank tea and smoked. The way to a Chinese patient's heart was an American cigarette.

Even in throes of illness these patients could not quite understand why the American nurses tended to their needs. They giggled when I checked a pulse rate; they thought it humorous that I would place a stethoscope on their chests to listen, and they had not the slightest idea what I was listening for. They watched every move I made, perhaps with distrust. Sometimes when I gave them medicine, they would take the tablets in their hands, and later walk all the way to Ledo to sell it to the local citizens who prized the quinine and the atabrine, for they too suffered from malaria.

One day, seven sick Chinese soldiers drifted into the hospital and were sent directly to my ward. They were suffering from dysentery, or *lï-jï*, as it was known to them. Everyone, at some time or other had a bout with dysentery, and if not properly treated it was severely debilitating. These men were dangerously dehydrated and needed infusions of plasma immediately. Routine use of intravenous therapy with glucose solutions was not used at this time in our overseas military units. I sent Wong, the ward boy, to assign each a *chwáng* and take their temperatures. He soon came running back to take me to their bedsides. They had, not knowing what a thermometer was, chewed the glass and little trickles of blood were running from the corners of their mouths. We yelled at them to spit out the glass, Wong in Chinese, I in English, making them look at us as though we were a couple of lunatics. It was times like this that I longed for my crispy little white cap, a row of beds made up with white sheets, and patients that reached out for the kind of care that nursing school had taught me to give. And as was usually the case, no infusions of plasma were available, so we settled for feeding them rice gruel and lots of water, and medicated them with paregoric and bismuth.

Patients with dysentery and malaria were always with us, and we treated them effectively. The disease that struck terror in the hearts of every American was mite-borne typhus. Sometimes the doctors diagnosed it as tsutsugamushi fever, or scrub typhus. For some reason, the Americans who contracted typhus were a great deal sicker than the Orientals who got it. Medical records confirmed the mortality rate in Caucasians was much higher than in the Chinese. During the battle to regain Northern Burma, the troops came down with mite-borne typhus at an alarming rate. We knew that rats were one of the vectors for this malady, which made living with those many rodents in our *bashas* very frightening. One of the doctors at the 14th Evac. became a good friend and taught me many things about the diseases we were seeing. He had not been in the theater as long as most other medical officers and was not suffering the erosion of spirit that prevailed, so he was more willing to respond to my calls for help. He came from Texas, so we called him Tex, Captain Tex.

It seemed that every day I went on duty a new problem confronted me. My heart ached for these poor soldiers, their frail bodies devastated by malevolent organisms, their hopes for a future dimmed by incessant warfare and inevitable poverty, their lives devoid of the good material things that we Americans took for granted. My tender feelings

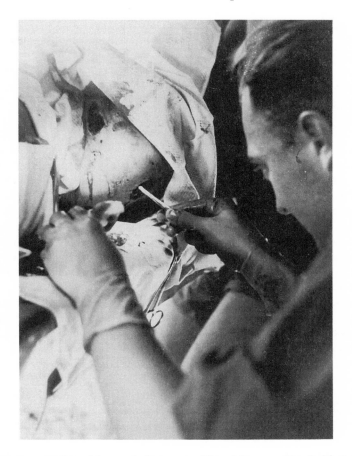

Cavernous wound requiring surgical treatment. The sulphas were all we had for infections.

could be, in an instant, replaced with fury, turning me into a screaming shrew. It was their spitting that did it. The Chinese are the greatest spitters on the face of the earth. When I saw a bolus of slimy, green mucous come flying through the air and land at my feet, I trembled with anger. *"Bu Hao! Bu Hao! Ting! BU HAO!"* (No good! No good! Listen! NO GOOD!) I knew that the sputum was more than likely to be loaded with tuberculosis bacilli since so many of the men had the disease. It was rampant in my ward. Spitting was not only uncouth, it was downright dangerous for us all. The only response I ever got from those little men, staring at me with eyes like obsidian, was laughter. No matter how angry or how discouraged I became, there was a quality in these Oriental soldiers that endeared me to them forever. Perhaps it was that they were much like children, forever seeking attention.

Another thing about Chinese soldiers—they laughed at everything, even things that were inhumane or cruel. Men from the airbase told of transporting troops who, when high over the mountains, pushed one of their fellow passengers out of the cargo bay door. He had become airsick and had leaned out of the opening to vomit, when another soldier gave him a shove and sent him hurtling earthward to certain death. They laughed, had a little sing-song harangue, and laughed some more. Actually, the Chinese penchant for laughter sometimes served a positive purpose and improved the morale of the troops when they were struggling against mud and mire and other impediments that soured the atmosphere.

On a wretchedly hot and rainy day, I sat in my stuffy little nurses' station watching the sheets of water pour off the wide overhang of thatch on the *basha*. I tried not to think about home, it was more comfortable to think about the here and the now. I looked forward to the later afternoon, that time of day when "Kismet" might sweep down from the mountains bringing that special message from the red-headed pilot who was beginning to be very interesting to me. His time was taken up seven days a week with flying responsibilities so he did not have many opportunities to come to the hospital. Sometimes, he was away for days and I had no way of knowing whether his plane may have cracked up on that cold, sinister Hump. Worry and dejection had settled on me like a shroud when the *basha* exploded into a barrage of gun-fire. I shot out into the ward expecting that a mortar shell had been dumped into the *basha*, or something equally as tragic, only to find that my patients were shooting at the cockroaches that crawled around the legs of the *chwángs*. They were wagering to see who could shoot the most roaches—they were enormous vermin—and laughing all the while they pursued their noxious enemy. I sent the ward boy to get Yang Jei-pen, the interpreter. He confiscated their weapons and we made a search of the entire ward to see just what ammunition was

stored there. Several of the patients had hand grenades in their clothing, side-arms were hidden in their shabby blankets, and there was a
large assortment of knives of various sizes and shapes, used, so they
said, for *wo yàu li-fà* (a hair cut). We could have had a war right there
in the *basha*, at the slightest provocation.

Chapter 7

Night Duty on the Ward

OUR CAPTAIN TRIED to arrange the nursing schedules so that everyone did her fair share of evening and night duty. Evening duty meant that we had no dates—no trips to Ledo to the Officers' Club. Our hospital had its own club, but without a band it just didn't stack up to the one at the airbase. Night duty was even more disconcerting than day duty. There was an eerie quiet over the wards at night, and the jungle conjured up all kinds of evil possibilities in my mind, even though there were a few guards posted around the area. Because the combat zones were now far from this part of the theater, the guards were not very serious about their surveillance: I once saw one of them sleeping soundly under the pole light in the middle of the compound. The best part of night duty was that it left the days free to do other things, like riding horses, sneaking off to the river for a swim—if you weren't terrified of the leeches that waited to latch onto your exposed parts—or getting someone to drive to one of the towns further down into the valley, or riding up to the Pangsau Pass into Burma.

My turn came to go on the night shift. Usually there was a leaden calm over the whole hospital enclosure by midnight. Unless the ward had acutely ill patients, the nurse in charge had much less work to do than in the daylight hours. After getting a report from the nurse who was winding up her shift, I always made rounds to ascertain firsthand the condition of each of the sick men. Because the Chinese were so reluctant to complain, it was easy to overlook a patient who was not responding well to treatment, or someone who was becoming febrile and had further need of special medication or infusions of plasma, which was always in short supply and usually reserved for our own men who were critical. The tropical diseases we were dealing with were unpredictable and of long duration. Sometimes a patient would appear to be well on the road to recovery, when suddenly his temperature would spike and he would become delirious, then the initially prescribed dosages of medicine were started all over again.

During the time when the battle casualties were high and the hospital short-staffed, the nurses had devised a clever way of hydrating those patients who needed it but were physically unable to drink fluids from a glass. They hung empty plasma bottles filled with distilled water over the patients' *chwángs*, then attached a length of tubing so the patient could drink without the help of the overburdened nurses.

Wong, the ward boy, always accompanied me on night rounds. Together we walked with flashlights down the long line of sleeping soldiers and I was able to point out those men who needed special attention. It was not easy to think of them as men, for they were more like children, small in stature, frail and thin. Most of them had, however, fought like men, courageously and hard, to defeat the Japanese in Burma. Unlike the patients, Wong was a very large Chinese, an attribute that he used to bully his fellow citizens into submission to his will. He ruled the roost, and even I was a little intimidated by his air of authority. Although I was very careful to ask him to do something in such a way that he felt he was my equal, I could not count on his doing it. Never did I see an ounce of compassion in his care of the men; even when one of them was dying, he handled him like a sack of potatoes. I always wished that Captain Williams would assign two of us to a ward, but she said there weren't enough nurses to do that.

We had a small supply of narcotics on each ward. I was told by the nurse who had been on night duty before me that it was not safe to leave these medications in the nurses' station, even though they were locked up. They had been stolen so many times that she resorted to carrying them in her pocket. I followed her example, but never felt quite comfortable walking around with morphine and codeine on my person. The Chinese soldiers' reputation for thievery was widespread, and for narcotics, notorious. Red has told me of finding the emergency kit in his plane stripped of every medication, including the contents of the morphine ampoules that had no evidence of having been disturbed but were bone dry.

The patients seemed to be comforted by the presence of a nurse in the long dark hours, and in their loneliness those who could walk about, often came into the nurses' station. With their pidgin English and my few singing Chinese phrases, we managed to communicate. The differences in our backgrounds was a wider rift than the strangeness of our languages. When the hospital was first established, the American soldiers and the Chinese were put in the wards together. The cultural abyss that yawned between Joe's bed and Wang's *chwáng* was so wide that they had to be separated immediately.

One night I came on duty to find all the ambulatory patients out of bed, standing in a group, yelling and cheering, while two patients fought in the center of the commotion. Each had a wicked looking knife poised for slicing up the other. Their faces were set with rage, their thin, agile bodies dancing an adagio of animosity, the knife blades glinting as they caught the light from the nurses' station.

"What's going on?" I asked the nurse whom I had come to relieve.

"Haven't found out yet. I sent Wong to get the interpreter, what's his name? Yang? I'm not about to step into that brawl."

"Any possibility that the new patients came from Yenan?" I was thinking that someone with Communist leanings might have triggered the altercation. Our Nationalist soldiers hated the Communists more than they feared the Japanese.

"I don't give a damn whether they kill each other or not. The more of these little bastards we can get rid of, the sooner we get back to the States." She was another one who was suffering from the pervasive breakdown in morale.

My chief concern was how to deal with this explosive situation. I was the officer in charge. Whatever happened, I was ultimately responsible and I had no stomach for a stabbing or a bloody laceration. If one of these men had to be sutured, I'd have a hard time getting a doctor to come at this time of night, and I had no equipment on the ward for doing it myself. It was a very unsettling situation. I had expected Wong, with his authority, would not permit such a display of hostility, but, there he was, at the ringside, flaming the fires of battle. "You skunk," I thought, "why are you allowing this to go on in my ward?"

Finally, Yang, our interpreter, came in and broke through the circle of excited on-lookers. He spoke to them with a controlled but powerful voice and succeeded in getting both angry men to hand over their knives. He ordered everyone back to his *chwáng*. Then he came into the nurses' station and sat down.

"Men fight over who get pajama with stripes," the interpreter said, his voice and manner dead serious. "It would be wise, Lieutenant, if United States make one kind pajama only. All with stripes or all plain color. It is too much controversy over who get pajama with stripes. This is important matter to soldier."

I was flabbergasted to think that pajamas could be cause for such a deadly contest. These men, these impoverished Chinese soldiers, had lived their lives with so pitifully little material advantages that a pair of pajamas was worth killing for.

While my night duty assignment lasted, the days were interminable. It was too hot to sleep during the day, and there were few other nurses for companionship. The monsoon rains continued; fat-bellied clouds ruptured and sent massive amounts of water falling over the already saturated forests. Then the sun would hold its hot face to the earth and the steam enveloped everything. By late afternoon it was usually safe to leave the *basha* without a poncho as the heaviest showers came in the middle of the day. It was easy to become dispirited when the physical discomfort of heat and humidity was so inescapable.

Chapter 8

Horseback Riding
in the Jungle

U P THE ROAD a few miles, was a British remount camp. I never
knew why there were horses there, but it seems that there has
always been a symbiosis of the British and their horses. Cavalry units
were commonly stationed in India, so more than likely they had been
deployed in the areas where there had been fighting. There were many
four-legged beasts of burden in the jungles, but these horses were
trained to be ridden. Mitzi had met one of the British officers, Tom,
and they were seeing each other quite regularly. Tom told me that the
horses in their unit were available to us for riding, if we cared to try.

Captain Tex and I drove up there one day and the Limeys (British
soldiers) gave us two beautiful geldings, saddled them, and wished us
a good ride. We headed out toward the Pangsau Pass into Burma. The
road had more curves than the snake on the Caduseus and rose increasingly upward, giving me the sensation of riding a horse straight into
heaven. The only thing visible was the narrow winding road under our
horses' feet and the distant towering mountains that seemed to belong
to another landscape. Below us, on either side, were mists and gray
vapors that hung over the jungle, covering the trees and the valleys
entirely. It was a feeling of being suspended in space. The road was
narrow, ribbon-like, with ruts close to the edges where the earth
dropped off into the clouds. The klop-klop of the horses' hoofs was
the only sound, then a whine penetrated the strange silence, first faint,
then building to a roar. I was certain that it was aircraft coming in. For
a minute I thought it might be Red, but the sound was not quite like
the comfortable drone that his C-47 made. Then I heard Tex yell, "Pull
over. It's a convoy!" The animal under me froze. He would not move

The author at a British remount camp near the Pangsau Pass into Burma. Horseback riding was a pleasant diversion.

in either direction. "Hurry up!" Tex screamed, but it was too late. The first two and a half ton truck of a long military convoy barreled around the curve ahead of us, followed by a long line of dirt-covered, olive drab monsters, chewing up the road and assaulting the silence of the lofty mountains. They were coming back from China where they had delivered their cargo, and their emptiness made it possible to travel at unreasonable speed. The drivers, some of them Chinese, hung one leg out the open door of the cab, ready to abandon the vehicle if it veered far enough to plummet over the side of the road. I couldn't see Tex. He was somewhere on the other side of the careening caravan. The mud and dirt flew up in every direction, obscuring the trucks and hiding me and the horse from the drivers' view. I wondered if we had been visible to anyone. The horse, trained to stand his ground in the midst of battle noises, had crabbed his way to the teetering edge of the road, planted his four feet firmly and waited for the noisy behemoths to pass. Tex had dismounted and held his steed by the halter. He broke into a huge grin when he saw me sitting in the saddle, badly shaken, but trying hard to hide my terror.

"I thought you were a goner," he said, patting my leg, then the horse's withers. "I think you would make a good Texan." He was used to women who understood horses; except for the beasts that pulled a plough, I knew nothing about horses or how to ride them.

There were not many convoys returning from China. Trucks that carried materiél over the Ledo Road into Kunming usually stayed there as Chiang Kai-shek was very eager to get as many vehicles as he could, for he too was surreptitiously planning for the inevitable conflict between the Nationalists and the Communists. As for getting the Japanese out of China, he expected the Americans to do that with a minimum of help from his army.

The Chinese drivers of the huge trucks on the road were both unqualified and unreliable, even though many of them were trained at Ramgarh for this particular job. One convoy, manned by Chinese, drove from Ledo toward Kunming. By the time they had reached the Pangsau Pass, thirty-eight miles away, their ninety vehicles had been reduced to only sixty-six that were operational. Many of them just ran off the road and dropped hundreds of feet into the jungle ravines.

Tex was becoming a problem. At first I believed that our common interest in the patients and the unusual diseases that we were learning about was the reason why he wanted to spend so much time with me on off-duty hours. Then I began to realize that he was developing an affectionate interest in me. That wasn't so bad—he was young, handsome, unmarried, and clearly a very good doctor. He loved Texas, horses and medicine, and I perceived that he was adding me to that list. I could easily have fallen in love with him, but it was really the "fly boy" who swooped over my *basha* at sundown, who triggered tachycardia in my youthful heart.

It was the height of the season for suffering. The moisture-laden air pressed down unrelentingly, wilting our spirits as well as everything else. It was hard to believe that when the 14th Evac. was first established, in the autumn of 1943, the nurses had suffered from the cold. They hovered over shock lanterns at night and were so paralyzed by the damp chill of the air in this mountainous land that they couldn't move their fingers to do the charting records. Patients went without baths because there was no way to heat water. The fuel shortage had been acute. My wildest imagination could not conjure up a scene of shivering while I sweated in today's one hundred degree heat, even though the ride up the mountain toward Burma brought a comfortable reduction in the temperature.

Chapter 9

A Visit with Red

THINGS IN THE THEATER were changing, and rumors flew around the hospital compound like ricocheting bullets. The combat zones were quiet after the battle at Myitkyina; there were a few enemy in the area, Japanese looking for a way to get back to their bases in China. We all felt that the war was changing and that we would eventually move to a place where we could care for the casualties that would follow an invasion of Japan. No one dared think of what that would be like, but neither did anyone think the Japanese would surrender. I found that it took all my energy just to get through each day and each night, so the rumors had little impact after the first wave of interest evaporated. I watched the sky for Kismet.

On another late afternoon my hopes materialized in a thunderous roar as Red's plane came out of the foggy sky to tree-top level. I hurried to change into fresh bush clothes, things that had been washed and pressed by the native laundry men, the *dhobi wallahs*. They used rice starch in the shirts and trousers they laundered, and the garments were as stiff as boards when first put on, then they became soft and sticky, wrinkled and messy. Something they used in the process made us break out with a rash. We called it *dhobi itch*. My neck was always adorned with a red ring of this annoying affliction.

My foot locker, government issue, contained all my worldly goods. I kept it under the cot for there was no room elsewhere in the *basha*. I pulled it out to see if there was some better looking khakis in it. My sister had given me an old evening gown that she no longer wore and because it seemed, at the time, such a windfall, I put it in the bottom of my locker, just in case. It was foolish even to own such a dress in this primitive environment. I looked at the folds of white jersey and the one red panel that ran down the front all the way to the floor-length hem, and remembered the dance at the New York Hospital, a party for the students. I had felt so elegant, so much a part of the world of adults when I dressed in that slinky long dress, but all that was on the other side of the globe. This was the hemisphere of rain, mud, heat, leeches, dysentery and a thousand other miseries. There was one bright spot: Red—and he'd be arriving in his jeep any time. I folded the dress and put it back in the foot locker. "Someday," I thought.

I can still see the smug smile of satisfaction on Red's face when he handed me a tin of chocolates that evening. The Whitman Candy Company had packed chocolates in vacuum sealed cans, especially for the people in the armed services. Vacuum packing candy was a new process in those years, but like many other ingenious ideas that came out of the war, it is still widely used in places where the climate is a threat to chocolate. For about ten minutes, I was the most sought after officer in the nurses' quarters. We had no such luxuries in our PX. We didn't even have the necessities. The limited supply of Kotex filled us with anxiety; we shared what we had with each other and pilfered the surgical dressings from the wards when we were destitute. Shortages of everything made it necessary to issue coupons for the right to purchase various items. Once I was able to buy a fountain pen, the perfect thing for someone who liked to write, as I did. Even pencils and paper were hard to get. I was keeping notes and storing them in a zippered briefcase, hoping one day to write an account of this Asian adventure. Before my tour of duty was finished, a sad misfortune befell my accumulation of notes, photographs, and my personal military records.

That night, we did not go back to the club at the airbase. Red and I sat in my *basha* and talked about places where we had been stationed and the events that had brought us here. I had learned that Red's real name was Arthur and that he had been born and brought up in New Jersey, not far from Manhattan where I had first worked as a professional nurse. He, like most all young men in their late teens, had enlisted in the military service, as this was a long and all-consuming war. The Classification Center in Nashville, Tennessee, had given tests to determine what role in the Army Air Force best suited him. He had, it appeared, the qualifications and the temperament to be a pilot. He had gone through a long list of schools, pre-flight training, primary flight, basic and advanced flight, all in places in the South East Training

Command, which covered the southeastern part of the United States. He had some hair-raising episodes in the months when he was learning to handle an aircraft, but nothing quite compared to the kind of flying that his work in the CBI entailed.

He told me about his involvement in a mid-air collision not long before he was awarded his wings. The students in his squadron were flying AT9s, a hot little training plane that was soon to be discontinued by the Hoover Commission because it was too dangerous. One day he was sandbagging (sitting in the copilot's seat) for another pilot as they practiced landings on a grass field. About five hundred feet above the ground he saw a shadow flash over the plexiglass cover of the cockpit. The fellow who was flying the aircraft was too busy to notice, but Red pushed the wheel with his knee in an attempt to fly under the plane that was directly on top of theirs. He felt the aircraft shudder and knew that something quite out of the ordinary had happened to the plane. The pilot brought the AT9 onto the field and they could see the other plane burning not far away. Both the pilot and the copilot of the other plane were injured, one with broken teeth and fractured bones, the other with no obvious wounds at the time of the collision, but after three days of normal activity, he was called back and advised that the x-rays taken showed he had a fractured femur! Both men survived.

I enjoyed listening to his accounts of flying, but while my ears tuned in to his words, my heart tuned in to something in his personage that held me spellbound. This was a time of critical passage in my life and I was groping for direction, trying to locate myself in my peer group, coping with turbulence that I could not explain. It was like being on a solo flight and not knowing how to operate the controls. Women had not been emancipated as completely as they are today; there were a lot of "shoulds" and "shouldn'ts" that governed our behavior. Even though I had achieved a profession, there was still the expectation of marriage and family, the accepted norm for my generation. So when I dated, I thought about men as possible choices for the long haul, and I always felt as though I were on trial for the same reason. Like many women in their early twenties, I had a romanticized version of men—they were brave, smart, reliable, chivalrous and more self confident than I would ever be. I studied every nuance in Red's expressions, and consciously revealed as little about myself as was possible. My origins were earthy and humble; I felt that he, like most men, would not be very interested in a girl with my country background.

Red's squadron of C-47s, the 317th Troop Carriers, was part of the 2nd Air Commando Group. There were also two squadrons of fighter planes in the group, and all were headquartered in Kalaikunda, a base near Calcutta. Sixteen C-47s and their crews had flown from the States, a long route from Florida to India, by way of San Juan, British Guiana, Brazil, then across the Atlantic. They stopped at Ascension Island then headed out for the Gold Coast of Africa. Across the wide dark continent they stopped to refuel at places such as Fort Lamey in French Equatorial Africa, El-Fashar in the Sudan, Khartoum, and on to Karachi in India. He and the other men in his squadron, like the personnel in the hospital units, had trained extensively in the States before going overseas. They had become a group bonded together with unwavering loyalty and firm commitment to each other. What happened to one man in the group became the concern of all the men, and when one plane and its crew was lost, it was as though members of a family had been killed.

Just as I had been catapulted out of rural Pennsylvania after a brief exposure to New York, Red had been propelled from his suburban world of North Jersey to strange lands and obscure places. We were both barely past our teen years, forced by the convulsions of war to grow up in a hurry, stretched out of provincialism by our nation's need to destroy our enemies on distant shores. I asked him about places he had been and if he had any idea where he would be sent after Ledo.

"The minute we touched down in Kalaikunda, we were ordered up to Sylhet," Red responded.

"Where's Sylhet?" I asked.

"It's just west of Imphal. We had to get supplies to the British, so they could keep pushing the Japs back down the Chindwin Valley."

"I heard about Imphal. I guess if the Limeys hadn't held fast there, the Japs would have come right on through to India." I was learning more and more about what had been going on in the CBI; about America's part in the war. The enemy had made a drive toward Imphal in the Indian state of Manipur, and had surrounded a garrison of British at Kohima, hoping to get a foothold on Indian soil.

Red then told me about General Stilwell's defeat:

"Imphal was the place where General Stilwell ended up when he walked out of Burma with that little band of people—there was a hand-ful of Americans, mostly officers, Dr. Seagrave and his Burmese nurses, some British—I don't remember who all there were, but the Japs were hot on their tails and they got out by the skin of their teeth. That was back in forty-two, before I got here. Funny thing about that was the news in the papers said the Americans and the British had a great vic-tory in Burma. Then Vinegar Joe, that's what they call Stilwell, spoke up and said 'I claim we took a hell of a beating.' Right then and there he decided that we had to take Burma away from the Japs, and that's why you and I are here right now." Red reached over and put his arm around my shoulder.

"Did we have troops in Imphal?" I asked.

"No, that was a British operation. They had always depended on the nature of Burma, its terrible mountains and disease-ridden jun-gles as a natural barrier to India, and were surprised when the Japs launched an attack toward Imphal and the Assam-Bengal Railway. General Wingate and his Chindits were dug in and ready to defend the supplies that the enemy wanted—you see, getting food and ammu-nition to an army fighting in this wild land was all but impossible. The Japanese, when they made the decision to break into India, sealed their fate because they were at the end of their jungle trails, mired in torrential monsoon rains, and had no food or supplies. Indian sol-diers, Gurkhas and more British were brought in to fight and they succeeded in routing the enemy. Our job was to fly in the troops, take out the wounded, carry ammunition and ordnance—even mules—but we had no combat troops in that battle. Support and supplies, that was what our country did for the British. It would have been a major catastrophe if the enemy had succeeded in fighting their way into India—might have been the collapse of the entire Southeast Asia Command. The Brits were in dire straits back home, everything going into defending their little island, so they needed our air power des-perately. When we got to Sylhet we were worked to death. Every day, seven days a week, we carried supplies to Imphal, Tulihal, Warazup, Myitkyina, and Monauk. Then we'd fly up this way to Chabua, Din-jan, Ledo—every day somewhere different. I'll tell you all about it someday." Red was looking around my *basha* while he tried to direct our conversation to something else. "So this is your home away from home."

"It must be the best *basha* in Assam, Red, because the rats just love it here. They tear up and down those framing poles all night."

"We live in tents down at the airstrip, and let me tell you, they get so hot inside you can't breathe until after sundown. These straw houses are much cooler, rats or no rats."

"Wish I could offer you a drink but I gave my liquor ration away."

Every officer was issued two bottles of booze a month, a commodity that I passed on to the enlisted men who did so much for us in the hospital. That was a violation of rules, but it seemed unfair that I should be given something that I cared nothing about just because I was an officer, when the enlisted men wanted liquor for their off duty relaxation. There was local gin, A & D for Assam Distilleries, and something called Bull Fight Brandy that the GIs had found to drink, but the medical officers warned against it because marijuana was one of its ingredients and those who imbibed became wild and irresponsible. I put my ration outside the *basha* and told an American medic to pick it up at his convenience.

"Let's have dinner." Red stood up abruptly, and I wondered if he thought I was going to cook a meal, or something equally ridiculous.

"You want to eat at our mess? You'll be sorry. Everything we have comes out of an olive drab can, and the cook has no imagination. You'll get Spam, fried potatoes and beans—the same thing every day since I've been here."

"There's a restaurant down the road," he said.

"You're kidding," I replied, thinking of all the dangers in ingesting local food. I pictured that dead fish, stretched out on a bowl of rice, that had been presented to me in the recent past. How could I believe that there was a restaurant out there in that dark, pathless jungle.

"I can get you back here in time to go on duty. C'mon. A lot of guys from the base eat at this place, and no one has died yet." He wasn't kidding, after all. Any change from fried potatoes and Spam would be a treat for me. We climbed in his jeep and headed downhill toward Ledo.

About halfway between the airbase and the hospital, the local

Chinese had established an eating place, testimony to their entrepreneurship. It was merely a shack, a thatched roof building, balanced on stilts, that straddled a deep gully. A wide plank stretched from the bank of the ravine to the entrance, leaving customers in peril should they make a misstep. Isolated, and without electricity, the establishment did a thriving business with personnel from the nearby airstrip and the hospital. Inside were little booths with curtains hung to give diners the privacy they liked. It turned out to be a great place to escape the monotonous menu at the 14th Evac., and the atmosphere was quiet and intimate. No one ever seemed to suffer from *li-ji* after eating their egg-fu-yung or chow-mein.

Never have I eaten a dinner in such a hovel, but in the smoky light of a sputtering oil lamp, I felt the glow of something new, a feeling that I could neither diagnose nor articulate. Perhaps it was just an infatuation for the personable young man who sat opposite me; maybe it was something more profound. Was it just that this remote place was conducive to romance, or was my loneliness making me vulnerable to the attention that he had been paying me? There was an uncomfortable feeling of being adrift, without the security of a familiar environment or the comfort of a family to lean on. In books and in movies, I had observed rapturous scenes of two lovers dining in elegance, while violins played and wine glasses tinkled. Here we were, eating eggs and bamboo shoots from a tin plate, chasing away wandering insects and wiping perspiration from our brows. A jungle paradise? Hardly. I didn't want to get wrapped up in someone I might never see again. There were many irrational and reckless affairs that developed between some of the nurses and the officers, relationships that probably collapsed when life returned to its normal cadence. I was awkward and quite unsure of myself where men were concerned and very conscious of my country background, trying desperately not to expose myself as the hick that I really was.

"Tell me more about the missions you've flown, Red." I sensed his reluctance to talk about where he flew and for what reason, but conversation of this nature was a way to avoid intimacy, something I didn't know how to handle. I wanted information about the war in the CBI so I could tell my folks about it when I wrote. They were vitally interested because I happened to be in this theater and there was always a dearth of information about the CBI campaign in the newspapers. A large portion of news came from the British press. By the time it was filtered through London it had lost much of the news about what Americans were doing.

"We flew to a lot of places behind the Jap lines. The OSS troops there had to be supplied rice and ammunition, and they still depend on the stuff we drop. When we first came to Ledo, we were out there every day—Bhamo, Lashio, Lawsawk. We flew down into the valley of the Irrawaddy to places like Mu-se, Warazup, and I made many trips to Myitkyina. We're still going over to Myitkyina quite regularly."

I told Red what I had learned about the 14th Evac. before I had been assigned there. "One of the nurses who went home when we came to replace the staff told me about the battle of Myitkyina. The patients poured in, men who had been wounded and those who had been sickened by the terrible fighting conditions in Burma. She said they were pitiful to see, half starved and exhausted. There wasn't enough room for these casualties so they added a lot of tents. There was no increase in staff so the doctors and nurses worked night and day to treat the men and get them back to decent physical condition. Sometimes the men were ordered back to the front before they were really ready to go, which made the doctors mad, but the field officers had the last word and Myitkyina had to be taken at all costs."

When the war was over, the insidious problem of morale in the theater was more openly discussed. There had been one organization whose bitterness was so great that they almost mutinied and an investigation ensued. This was the combat force known as Merrill's Marauders, made up of veterans of action in the Pacific, and some rough characters who were poorly disciplined but had a dare-devil spirit. They had responded to General Stilwell's call for men to perform a hazardous mission, to get behind the Japanese lines in Burma and isolate the enemy army that had infiltrated the jungle. Their first order was to seize Walawbum in the middle of Burma, but to get there they marched for sixty miles in monsoon rains, knee-deep mud, malarial infested swamps, and with constant fear of the lurking enemy at every turn. Air support was almost non-existent because the pilots could not see where to drop supplies. Hunger was added to all the other miseries. They fought for five days, side by side with Chinese troops, to capture Walawbum, then were pinned down for eleven days at Nphum Ga. They referred to this battle as "Maggot Hill" because the dead mules and the decomposing bodies of their own casualties were crawling with maggots. The only water they could get was contaminated by all the necrotic tissue around the stream, and they could not even raise their heads as the enemy responded to every move with bullets. After they had finally driven the Japanese away from the hill, they expected to be returned to Ledo, but Stilwell ordered them on to Myitkyina to take the airstrip there. They were in awful condition—limping with sore feet, hungry, exhausted, filthy, so overcome with dysentery that some of them had cut the seat of their trousers away so as not to be hampered in combat. The final straw was when Stilwell ordered the convalescents in the hospital back to the field. The nurses and the medical officers were infuriated too, but there was nothing they could do.

While we finished eating, we talked about the Burma campaign. Usually conversation turned to expectations for going home, and these hopes were beginning to look pretty good, but I was becoming concerned that going home would be a permanent separation from Red before I got to know him. We continued to share our experiences in this obscure military action in a global war.

"One of the most important jobs we had was dropping the paratroopers on Rangoon," Red told me.

"Tell me about it," I asked eagerly.

"Not now. Don't have time. I've got to get you back to the hospital, you know. If you're not at your post on time, that chief nurse of yours will blame it on me." He got up and pulled the curtain in the booth, then came back and sat down next to me. He leaned over and a kiss melted on my lips. It was a tremulous moment. I felt smashed. Neither of us said anything but I felt my heart, laced tight in ribbons of inhibition and protocol, straining to loosen those bonds. We left the building, carefully picked our way over the plank that spanned the gully and got back into the jeep.

Driving back to the hospital that night we talked more about how our lives had become entangled in the war and how all the people our age were somewhere far from home trying to get the whole thing behind us. He told me of men in his squadron who crashed into the mountains, the peaks shrouded in gray clouds, and that the charts they used were very inaccurate.

Eventually, I learned even more about his involvement. The

British forces, fighting on the Arakan Coast hoped to begin a northward climb and get rid of the Japanese altogether. They called on the air commandos for a parachute drop of eight hundred Gurkha soldiers on Rangoon. The Gurkhas were the elite of the British Indian Army. They came from Nepal where the mountainous terrain spawned a special kind of physical endurance. Not only did these highly disciplined soldiers fight in Asia, they joined the British in the European theater where they were known for their bravery and endurance in the face of insurmountable dangers. Hand to hand combat and guerrilla warfare were their specialties. Each Gurkha carried a kukri, a knife with a long curved blade with the cutting edge on the inside curve. This weapon, in addition to the firearms supplied by the military, made this adaptable soldier, one of the most formidable fighting men that every existed. In Europe they were reported to have stolen noiselessly into German fox holes and decapitated the enemy with one stroke of that lethal weapon.

Red's squadron, the 317th Troop Carriers flew to Akyab to load the Gurkhas for the invasion of Rangoon. They had a very brief rehearsal back in Kalaikunda, and from that dry run the story was told that one of the Gurkha soldiers went forward to the cockpit to talk with the pilot. He was concerned that at an altitude of 800 feet the jump appeared to be too dangerous for his men. He made the humble request that the pilot bring the plane down to about half that altitude when he unloaded the soldiers.

"But at that low altitude there won't be time for the 'chutes to open," the pilot explained to the Gurkha.

"Oh," came the reply. "I didn't know we were going to wear parachutes."

That morning in Akyab, the crews were awakened at four in the morning for briefing. Their cargo bays filled with Gurkha paratroopers, they flew directly south, over the Bay of Bengal and turned east to Elephant Point, on the same latitude as their drop zone near Rangoon. They unloaded their cargo of paratroopers without a hitch, but to everyone's surprise the Japanese had withdrawn, leaving these scrappy little soldiers with no one to fight.

"Flying in that area was nothing like flying in the mountains between here and China, and it looks as though most of our traveling will be north from here on," he said. "A lot of those mountains are a hell of a lot higher than the maps indicate. Sometimes we just feel our way through the fog and the rain and hope to God we're on the right course."

"Did you ever get lost or have a mountain rise up in front of you—ever scared?" I asked.

"I had a close one, a few months back. We had old Kismet loaded with pipe, I mean loaded! We had to take it over to Myitkyina where we had flown dozens of times. It was a milk run for me and the crew. We just set the course and the time, lifted off and when we got there, looked for a hole in the sky. We had done this for days in a row, but this time, when we found the opening in the clouds and started to make our descending circle, something didn't look right. There's a bend in the Irrawaddy that we've used as a landmark ever since we started flying to Myitkyina. From that bend, it's easy to see the airstrip. Old Dick, my crew chief knew something was wrong. He knew the territory like the back of his hand, and he could tell that it wasn't the right bend. Right river, wrong bend. There were high jagged peaks standing just off our wing tips. We were down in a hole, mountains in every direction. I started to circle. If we could climb out of the hole we'd be okay, but the damn plane was so overloaded with pipe that I couldn't gain any altitude. I nosed the plane upward and opened the throttle as much as I dared."

All the while Red was telling me these things, the jeep was swinging around one curve and then another, making so much noise I had to lean over toward him to hear what he was saying.

"Dick was standing in back of me and the copilot, his eyes glued to the altimeter. The more circles we made and the longer he could see that we were not gaining any altitude, the whiter his face got. There was dead silence in the plane."

"And then?" We were shaking around like loose nuts and bolts as the jeep clattered over the rough road. I was glad there was no one else on the road. Rarely did we meet another vehicle as we drove between the hospital and the airstrip.

"I knew that if I could widen the circle by flattening out the wings, we might be able to climb, but the mountains were so close that I wasn't sure I could scrape through. Hey, we were all sweatin' this one out. We were concerned, too, that circling around as we were, our gas was being consumed and we might have to bring Kismet down in some rice paddy

Red (Arthur Camp) and the jeep that traveled often from the airbase to the 14th Evac. Hospital.

if we did get out. Even that was a better option than running into those rock-solid peaks that loomed above us. Round and round we flew until finally, after what seemed forever, the altimeter showed we were beginning to lift ourselves out of that predicament. If we had been able to jettison some of the pipe—but it was wedged in the plane so tight there was no way of throwing it out. It was a close one. I'd be lying if I said I wasn't scared. There'll probably be more close calls before we get out of here."

"Did you ever figure out how you got off course?"

"Never did. The only thing we could think of was that there was a wind from the south that blew us up river about fifty miles. The further north you fly, the higher the mountains get, and flying blind in the rain and the fog is what really makes your palms sweat. We lost good men in those deadly mountains."

"Do you have to haul any more of that pipe?" I asked. I visualized his C-47 crammed full of lengths of gray metal and unable to lift the load over the bleak peaks that held those unfortunate fliers in the cold silence of eternity. I was hoping he wouldn't have to transport any more of that heavy stuff.

"No, the pipeline is almost finished. Next week I have to go down to Calcutta. Wanta go?" he asked. I thought he might be teasing, but he wasn't kidding about the restaurant so there was a chance he was serious.

"I'll ask the captain if she can spare me." I was thrilled.

"Just ask for a three day pass. Don't tell her where you're goin," Red said, as he turned off the road onto the spur that ended near my *basha*. He had more experience with commanding officers than I had. I think his philosophy was to do what you wanted to do first and ask permission later.

I heard him whistling softly, "Darling, Je Vous Aime Beaucoup" as he climbed back in the jeep. The pale disc in the heavens lighted the sleeping hospital compound, spreading a shining luster over the narrow, crooked paths that wound from one thatched roof building to the other. I hurried through the splendor of the Indian night to my assigned post, the ecstasy of that gentle kiss still sweet upon my mouth.

While I went about my nursing duties, walking on the mud-packed floor felt like dancing on a cloud. All the while I gave care to the very ill, medications and treatments designed to bring these wounded and sick men back to health, my brain was formulating a way to ask Captain Williams for time off so I could accept Red's invitation to go to Calcutta. My spirit soared.

Chapter 10

A Trip to Calcutta

T EX CAME TO my *basha* to invite me to go riding again. It was his favorite thing to do, and although I enjoyed going off into the wild countryside, the frightening experiences I had cooled my enthusiasm for riding horses. After nearly being swept from the narrow trace of the Ledo Road into a gaping jungle ravine by an oncoming convoy of cowboying military trucks, I had another fright when my horse saw an elephant working in the jungle. He laid back his ears and tore out to the remount camp at full gallop while I clung like a limpet to the saddle. I was stretching my luck and was inclined to put off riding until we could saunter through the tea plantations further back to the west of Ledo. This was the perfect way to spend an evening, watching the sun go down in roseate glory and the moon rise to cast lacy shadows over the green, glossy tea plants. But Ledo was nineteen miles away, and the plantations even further.

"Thanks anyway, Tex, but it's too hot for riding and I've been invited to go to Calcutta. I have to get my gear together for that," I explained.

"You have a mission there?" Tex inquired.

"Not exactly. One of the pilots I met down in Ledo asked if I'd like to go with him. He has to go for supplies for the airbase, and Captain Williams gave me a three day pass, so I'm off. Out of the mud and slime for a day or two."

"I see." Tex was crestfallen, and I felt a bit guilty, flying off with Red.

Tex and I were great friends and he had been very helpful to me when I needed medical service for my Chinese patients. He never refused my requests and was genuinely interested in the well-being of the Chinese, which was more than I could say for many of the other physicians. I also sensed that he was on the verge of making his amorous intentions known to me and expecting some positive response.

"Well, have a good time," he muttered as he stooped to leave the *basha*. Once outside he hesitated, then turned and stuck his head back in. "Hey, please don't get stupid and fall for that fly boy."

I had never been inside Kismet, but I had flown in other C-47s, so I knew what to expect: bucket seats, banged-up metal floors, stretchers stored against the ribbed walls of the cargo bay, overhead wires used for paratroopers. What I hadn't expected was the odor. It smelled so vile when I entered I thought this sturdy old plane would rise ten feet off the earth before the engines even started.

"Red," I gasped, "I don't want to seem ungrateful for a ride to Calcutta, but is there something or someone dead in the belly of this thing?" I was holding my hand over my nose.

"Let me explain," he said, his olfactory nerves apparently immune to the stifling atmosphere. "We've been carrying Chinese to Chanyi, and also their mules. There's probably some rice in the belly, grain that has found its way down there from the food drops to the OSS men. The mules urinate in the plane and I guess it drips down there and in this heat the rice ferments. I apologize. I promise to see what I can do about getting rid of the smell as soon as I have time."

"I didn't know you carried mules," I said, thinking that I'd reek disgustingly by the time we got to Calcutta.

"Mules are a very important beast in this campaign. There are not many roads where wheeled vehicles cannot travel but mules can carry heavy loads into the mountains, through the mud and up and down those rocky ravines. We just put some bamboo poles inside the plane and tie the critters to them. Each mule has his own Chinese muleteer to help keep it under control."

"Where'd these mules come from?" I asked.

"They were shipped here, a lot of them, from the States. Big ol' Missouri mules. One time while we were flying over the Hump, just floating along, all of a sudden I felt the plane stop in midair. It was the damnedest sensation. It stopped, then jerked forward, then did the same thing again. The copilot and I were baffled, until someone from the back came up and told us that one of the mules had gone berserk. I went to the rear to see for myself and found that the animal was wild, kicking so violently that the muleteer was holding a pistol ready to

Kismet, the trusty C-47. This plane was used in all theaters during World War II.

shoot. He'd kicked out the ducts in the ceiling. We sure didn't want to crack up because of the frenzied behavior of some jackass, but just then he calmed down and they didn't have to shoot him after all."

We left the airstrip at Ledo in the early morning. Besides Red and me, there was the copilot, the radio-man and the crew chief. There were always these four people aboard the cargo planes, and sometimes a navigator, but generally the pilots did their own navigation. They had loaded a jeep into the cargo bay for transportation after we arrived in Calcutta. That struck me as being the epitome of luxury, having a jeep rolled out of the plane for our own means of getting around in all these strange places on a far continent. We didn't have to find the motor pool, requisition a jeep, then sign it out and be concerned about returning it when we were ready to leave.

Calcutta was about six hundred miles from Ledo by air. As we flew to the southwest the Patkai Range was off to the port side of the plane, then other hills appeared, but none of those towering giants that forced your heart into your mouth. The summits were clothed in heavy jungle growth, and as the land gradually leveled off into the great flood plain that is Bengal, we could see Kismet's shadow on the earth beneath. This wide flat land gets the overflow of both the Ganges and the Bramhaputra rivers, and much of the time there is an inland sea covering the silt of this enormous delta. One of the thousands of waterways that wind through this immense wedge of land, looking from the air like the intricate human vascular system, is the Hooghly River. I had sailed up that river months before, where thirty miles of Calcutta's misery meets the water at the river's edge.

When I had left the USS *Freeman*, earlier in the year, I was concerned about where I'd be stationed, and spent only a little time exploring this infamous city. I had never heard anyone say anything nice about Calcutta, but from the hospital where they billeted us for those few days, it didn't appear to be entirely bad. This brief visit to the city would expose me to some of the truths of this most monstrous accumulation of human woes.

No living soul can escape the sodden, smothering climate of this sprawling city in the middle of July. It presses down, it forces your sweated garments to cling, and the moisture and heat work a poaching process on your body, leaving you limp and listless. Mark Twain, when he visited Calcutta, said: "The weather was enough to make a brass doorknob mushy."

For some reason Red could not land at Dum Dum, the most heavily used airfield in the area, so he set the plane down on a small airstrip in Alipore, one of the southern suburbs of this extensive metropolis. We saw no Americans there, but a Royal Air Force officer greeted us and told us not to be fooled by his uniform, that he was indeed an American who had been in India working for an oil company when the war broke out. He promptly joined the RAF and had been on active duty there for a long time; in fact, he hadn't been home for seven years.

"Where's home?" Red asked.

"I'm from a little town in New Jersey, Glen Ridge. Probably you never heard of it," he commented.

"Fact is," Red replied, "I hail from Bloomfield." These towns were, and still are, adjacent to each other. They had a good visit talking about places that were familiar to both of them. I would have reason to be glad I had met this young man, for sometime in the following year, after I was mustered out of the service, a remarkable coincidence found me nursing his father in a hospital in New Jersey.

The crew chief and copilot put the ramp up to the door and Red guided the jeep out of the cargo bay onto the airstrip. Driving into town was instant exposure to the extremes of poverty and wealth, both existing in the shadow of each other, everyone averting his eyes from what

Mules used in jungle warfare. The terrain in Burma was so forbidding that only mules could be used to carry ordnance.

he did not want to see. The activities in the streets of Calcutta seemed to me a mindless, noisy confusion. Thousands of people walked, ran, squatted and lay on and in the streets. Sacred Brahman cattle strolled nonchalantly in front of cars, even on the tram tracks. Sikhs, who are the traditional taxi drivers, kept up an incessant din of horn blowing, adding to the noise of rickshaw drivers ringing little brass bells. Then the ubiquitous beggars, crying "baksheesh, baksheesh, no mama, no papa, baksheesh," followed the jeep and stretched forth their pleading hands whenever the vehicle slowed.

Red was trying to find Chowringhee Road, one of the main streets, and from there we were looking for the 142nd General Hospital where I could stay while enjoying my three-day pass.

"I hope I don't run into one of these sacred cows," Red remarked as he swerved to avoid a languid, almond-eyed beast, chewing on his cud and standing in the middle of the road.

"I hope you don't hit one of those beggars brushing against the side of the jeep," I added.

"Well, you know the Indian government will fine me twenty rupees if I hit a cow; ten, if I run down a pedestrian."

That schedule of fines was clearly understood by all our military people in India. It represented a value system that flew in the face of everything I had ever been taught, as a child, as an adolescent growing up in what I thought was a poor community, and as a nurse who valued human life above all things.

The British in India had established a rhythm of life that was easy to fall into. Insulated from reality, theirs was a world of clubs, tennis, polo, and servants to wait upon them for almost every human activity. They had become soft and self-indulgent, had forced an entire country to be subservient to their innate feelings of superiority. The system that perpetuated poverty was not necessarily the fault of the British, for the caste system, which allows the exploitation of all men, in the guise of religion, had a deadly grip on the people. Had it not been for England, I wonder whether there would ever have been railroads, schools, hotels or businesses in the subcontinent. One of the most striking features of Indian life, whether wealthy or destitute, in the big cities or in the country, is a lack of community responsibility. Without that ingredient, none of those institutions is possible. In an indefinable way we could sense the anger of the masses, a rage that would eventually spawn a bid for independence. We heard a murmur that would rise to a shriek before we left India.

The officers' quarters at the 142nd General Hospital had plenty of spaces for visitors. I noticed that some of our medical personnel lived in palaces with marble floors and beautiful gardens. "Maybe," I thought, "when we all come down out of Assam and Burma, we'll be stationed here." I signed into a room in a barracks built especially for personnel who worked at the hospital, and peeled off my bush clothes. My dress uniform packed in the musette bag, was a mess of wrinkles but a servant took it to be cleaned and pressed and returned it in less than an hour. I had heard that you could get a whole new uniform made in less than a day. It appeared that the entire Indian population was geared to waiting hand and foot on Europeans and Americans.

It is only in retrospect that I realize there were only flickers of profound thought that flashed through my brain when I was twenty-one. I was just practicing adulthood, gathering little wisps and threads of information that would add to my grownup stature. In this sea of new experience, I was focused on the red haired guy with the cap pushed back on his head, not on abstract issues like justice and human rights. We left the jeep at the barracks where I was billeted and climbed into a rickshaw, to be carried to the Great Eastern Hotel for dinner. I winced at the sight of a human being straining to carry two able-bodied Americans to feast on a meal that would never be available to him in his lifetime. The sweat trickled over his taut muscles. Bare feet, splayed from the weight of heavy burdens and from never having known the protection of shoes, stepped surely and swiftly over the streets, dodging the traffic of other rickshaws, automobiles, cows, and people. Near the entrance of the hotel beggars begged, men slept, and what looked like an abandoned pile of rags stirred to reveal yet another human being. The *durwans* (doorkeepers) were never able to keep the hotel verandah clear of street people, for like flies, their swarming was ceaseless. Red paid the rickshaw puller a rupee even though the British advised us that two annas was the standard fee for a rickshaw ride—one anna was a sixteenth of a rupee.

Military personnel, some from the Army, some from the Navy, British, Americans, Chinese, Indians and others I could not recognize filled the hotel dining room. Turbaned servants padded noiselessly around the tables while the *punkas* moved the air over the diners. The essence of elegance, fading along with the British empire, was pervasive. We were a very inconspicuous couple in that milieu. We sipped gin gimlets, sealed off the world that churned around us, and slipped into that ecstasy of wooing that was a high priority activity in our age group. As always, our conversation pivoted around the life we hoped to resume when the war was over.

The next day, Red gathered the supplies that he had to carry back to Ledo, and we found time to walk around the Maidan, a large open park in the center of the heavily populated area of the city. We crossed the Hooghly and visited the giant Banyan tree which towers eighty-eight feet, has a circumference of twelve hundred feet made up of six hundred roots. Throngs of men and women moving about boggled my mind by their very numbers. We were having such a lark: getting away from our primitive existence in the wet hill country of Assam, having dinner in something other than the officers' mess, holding hands and talking about the inevitable return to our stateside lives, trying to make the right impression on each other. We were experiencing those intense emotions of youth.

"We've got to go over to our headquarters in Kalaikunda and pick up some documents before we head home," Red informed me.

"It's okay with me, just as long as I get back on time. I'd hate to be AWOL." I think our captain would have felt personally responsible if anything happened to one of her nurses, especially one of the younger girls.

At Kalaikunda, there was an atmosphere of dejection among the officers whom Red talked with. There had been a most unfortunate calamity there recently. The two fighter squadrons in this group were headquartered there and had been keeping their spirits nourished with some wild flying. One of the men was horsing around, trying to see just how hot his P-51 was. He took the plane up about ten thousand feet with the idea of buzzing the field. He made a perpendicular dive, pulled out when the plane was barely off the ground and flew low over a ramp where two Gurkha soldiers were standing guard. The approach was at such speed that the Gurkhas could not react quickly enough. One of them threw himself on the ramp, but the other, having heard the roar of the engine, raised his arm to shield his eyes. It was too late. The propeller sliced off his face and his arm. It was a tragedy that was discussed with great shame, for the Americans had an intense admiration for the Gurkha soldiers. The U.S. government paid the victim's family a sum of money, and the pilot who was responsible was transferred out of the squadron.

It was no hardship to leave the climate in Calcutta, to exchange the putrid odors of the street for the musty smells of the jungle, to escape the crush of the numberless men and women whose suffering has no end. Although we had enjoyed ourselves, we felt more at home in the bush than in the city.

And I had the haunting feeling that I had done exactly what Tex asked me not to do.

Chapter 11

Shopping for Boots
with a British Colonel

M ITZI WAS GLAD to see me when I got back. "Let me give you the bad news first," she said. "Ingrid's sick. Critical."

"Typhus?" I asked. It was alarming to hear that one of our own had possibly fallen victim to this most feared malady of the jungle. We had all had bouts of dysentery, a few of the women had malaria, and I knew of one nurse who had been discharged with active tuberculosis, but among the nurses who now staffed the hospital, no one had contacted anything as life-threatening as typhus.

Ingrid was loved by all of us, perhaps because she seemed so physically fragile. She was a Scandinavian, platinum blonde with skin so white that you could see the tiny blue veins at her temples. Atabrine had turned her skin such bright yellow that her hair looked more gray than blonde. Ingrid was really dedicated to the profession, never leaving a stone unturned in search of ways to make patients comfortable. She rarely joined in the fun of any event but remained on the exterior of our camaraderie, cool, rigid and remote. We used to refer to her as Florence Nightingale, not to her face, but among ourselves.

"No one said it was typhus," Mitzi said. "They're calling it an FUO (fever of undetermined origin)." That was a diagnosis that the doctors used to cover a lot of the acute infectious diseases that were not clearly identifiable. When a patient came to us with any or all of these symptoms: chills, elevated temperature, tachycardia, severe headache, muscle and joint pain, vomiting, and often delirium, we had to put some name on his misery, and FUO was as good as anything, until the laboratory could identify the organism responsible for his illness. There recently had been several cases of "relapsing fever" among our staff, and

Ingrid's symptoms sounded familiarly like theirs. Along with other vermin, body lice were vectors for this spirochetal infection but surely she didn't have lice. Again I thought about those evil rats that made their homes in our *bashas*, and probably lice made their home in the fur of those dirty rodents.

"The good news is that you're scheduled to go back on day duty. You're to take over Ingrid's ward."

The next thing I heard was that Ingrid had been evacuated to the 20th General Hospital in Ledo where they had some air-conditioned places for the very sick patients. From there she would be sent down to Calcutta and when strong enough, back to the States by air. I recalled how we used to tease this girl: She was on the USS *General H. B. Freeman*, the liberty ship that had brought us to India. Whenever Ingrid walked into the officers' mess on that tedious sea voyage across the Pacific, down under Australia and through the Indian Ocean, we would all rise, and, in our best guttural Swedish accents, shout in unison, "Eeengreed Yohnson, from Minneeesota, eata plentee brrrread." A rose-colored blush would rise in her alabaster cheeks, making her even more exquisite than she already was. Although this was done in the spirit of fun, it was easy to see that this shy and timid nurse felt embarrassed by such antics.

I was glad to go back to day duty but wasn't thrilled with the idea of having a whole new *basha* of Chinese patients to contend with, a whole new set of musical names to remember, a new schedule of daily patient care routines. This was a rehabilitation ward, mostly men who had sustained serious injuries during the combat in Myitkyina. They would never be able to return to military service, but our goal was to prepare them as best we could for a functional life back in their own nation. There were many amputees and paraplegics, and sometimes, the infections and parasitic diseases that ravaged other patients, were superimposed on these men with skeletal handicaps. I didn't want to think of what life would be like for them and their families when they left the American hospital.

Their reluctance to leave was evidenced by cleverly disguised malingering when they appeared before the military board that decided the disposition of each case. Evacuating them back to China was delayed by the lack of space in aircraft; ground travel was made difficult by inadequate facilities for transporting disabled patients; and in any event, aside from the Ledo Road, there was no way to get over the mountains to China, except to fly. Their own officers didn't seem to be as concerned for the well-being of their men as the nurses were, but we had all become aware that these attitudes were one of the obvious differences in our cultures. While they waited to leave the hospital, it was important to keep them occupied. Many of the men liked to work with a needle and thread; they mended uniforms and sewed patches over worn out knees and elbows. The nurses assigned simple ward tasks to them and their willingness to perform was genuinely appreciated by all of us. I tried to impress on these men that spitting was unacceptable, but they continued to spit and they laughed at me for being offended.

"Hope you liked Calcutta," Mitzi said "because that's where we're sure to go when the 14th closes." I told her about the wonderful flight down there and about our dinner at the Great Eastern.

"You sure got lucky, finding a date with an airplane. The rest of us feel like we're stuck. I'm going shack-wacky and must get away from here, even if it's for only a day, so Tom and I are driving over to Tinsukia on Saturday. Interested?" Mitzi asked. She and Tom liked to browse around the little villages in the area. Sometimes they would run into British or Scottish people there who enjoyed conversations with Americans. These Europeans had come to Assam to exploit the one commercial product of the region, tea. I came to feel that the whole world adored anything or anybody who came from the United States. We all felt very smug about being American, perhaps because everyone looked upon our nation's wealth with envy. Ours was the country of the "haves" and we were deeply involved in the world of the "have nots," and even though I am reluctant to admit it, I must confess that most of us were less than gracious in our dealings with the non–European natives. We referred to them as "wogs" or "gooks" in the self-righteous belief in western omnipotence and personal superiority. At the same time, we were wholly and earnestly dedicated to ridding the globe of Hitler and Tojo who had brought the afflictions of war to everyone's doorstep. The Second World War was costing our country much, but we were not bled to death or brought to ruin as other countries were. It was not until after the war that we became the super power that we have been for the past four decades.

"If I'm not scheduled to work, I'll go," I agreed.

"There's a colonel up at the remount camp who wants a date with an American girl. I told Tom I'd ask you if you were available." Mitzi looked at me hoping I'd agree to go, then she asked, "You serious about what's-his-name, Hot Shot Charlie?"

"He's okay. I think I could get to like him a lot, only I'm afraid it might be just one of those crazy war romances that falls flat when things get back to normal. What looks good out here in the jungle may look ridiculous in Pennsylvania. Mitzi, I'm so homesick I could die. I hope all this attention I'm getting isn't an ambush, but when he's around I don't have that gnawing hunger for home. Maybe that's why I like him so much. Then there's Tex—I guess he's given up chasing after me, but I do like him." I was beginning to understand how brief and how brittle relationships could be.

"Tex doesn't have an airplane, remember?" Mitzi said.

"What a reason to date a guy." I sighed.

"Over here it's a darn good reason," she chuckled.

If I'd tried to reconstruct a map for my life, there was no place to put this haunting gap where I felt so displaced, so uneasy about all the crumbling idealism that surrounded our little group of professional men and women.

"Buck up, Vonny. We're all homesick, but this war won't last forever. The patient census is dropping off fast now, so we may be nearer home than you think. Being so far back in the woods in this awful climate is what really gets to me—not the work, I like the 'slopies' (another term widely used to describe the Chinese). Wait 'til you get a ward full of brass to take care of. They are the worst patients in the world—arrogant, demanding, and hung up on military chickenshit." Mitzi had a penchant for seeing the world in real terms. I was more unrealistic and dreamy about things. But she could make me feel better about our situation because she always felt that things would change, that something wonderful was right around the corner.

Mitzi had been dating Tom, a British officer, for months. He was a lanky, starved looking fellow with the gentle manners of an English farmer, which is exactly what he was.

"I absolutely adore that big old Tom, but I'll bet he has a wife and kids back in Yorkshire," Mitzi confided.

"Do you think he'd be seeing you every night if that were the case?" I was much too naive to think that someone who was married would latch onto another woman, but I later learned that it happened with predictable regularity.

"What the hell! I'm not even going to think about that." Mitzi took things as they came and made the best of every situation. She knew that Tom would go back to England and that she would never see him again, but she was going to enjoy his company while he was here. "How about it—a date with the British colonel? Tinsukia has a few bazaars where the Muslim Indians sell leather goods and I want to get a pair of CBI boots." Hindus never have anything to do with cowhide or leather products, as these animals are sacred to them.

I agreed to Mitzi's proposal. I, too, wanted to get those boots that were perfect to wear in the mud and muck of the jungle, for they covered the ankles as a protection from leeches that were ever present in the grass and foliage. Those ugly leeches—they came in sizes from a half inch to over four inches long—could attach themselves and become engorged with blood before you were aware of their presence. Holding the lighted end of a cigarette to the loathsome bloodsucker was the only effective way to detach it after it had begun gorging itself. The boots we hoped to buy had CBI patches sewn on the outside surfaces, they were easy to slip into and out of, and everyone from buck private to general wore them.

I sat down to write to my folks. They would love hearing about my escapade in Calcutta, and I wanted them to get a vivid picture of real poverty, not the kind of poor that our farming community understood. Visions of home crept into my mind as I wrote. It was time for the strawberries to ripen back on the farm. Oh, how I would love to have had a bowl of those delicately delicious berries. Memories of Mom's strawberry shortcake swimming in cream from our own golden Guernsey cows sifted into my brain. I tried to picture everyone at home doing the things they had always done, looking the way they had always looked, but for some reason everything seemed out of focus. I no longer felt like a part of my own family but like a nomad without a permanent abode. Letters that I mailed home couldn't possibly convey the truth of my situation for there was no way I could describe the feelings of isolation and longing that roiled inside. Sitting there in my *basha*, spasms of yearning overtook me, but I rarely resorted to crying as I had seen some of the nurses do.

Occasionally one of the girls would begin to unravel and we all descended upon her with the kind of attention she needed. We craved fresh vegetables but dared not touch them for they were fertilized with human excrement. Fresh fruit was never available except for an occasional pineapple that grew in the vicinity. Most everything that was edible was so contaminated that it was better to eat only our own American rations and the food that came from cans. We often talked of the day when we could eat salads and fresh food, and the longer we were in India the greater became our hunger.

Tom and the colonel came to our *basha* early in the morning. When I was introduced, my first thought was, "A genuine, unabridged Limey." He was much older than I, dignified, and ram-rod straight. He had been in the theater since the beginning of the war and felt as much at home in India as I felt in the rolling hills of the eastern United States. His stiffness and reserve carried over to his speech—clipped, precise, and to my ears, unintelligible. The brush mustache on his upper lip moved spastically with each little grunt or syllable, and I had a terrible time trying to figure out what he was saying. I kept asking, "What was that, sir?" or "What did you say, sir?"

We climbed into the jeep and headed away from the hills, down toward Ledo. At Ledo, they were erecting a new sign that renamed the road, "The Stilwell Road" in honor of the feisty little general who had, with dogged determination, accomplished the building of this passage that broke the Japanese blockade of China. The sign gave the number of miles from the road's starting point in Ledo to significant places along the 1,079 miles to its terminus in Kunming. It joined the old Burma Road at Lungling to the west of Kunming. It took twenty-four days of rough driving for a convoy of trucks to drive that length. We stopped to get a good look at the new landmark and took some photos.

Mitzi and Tom were happily engaged in conversation up in the front seat. I was trying to loosen up the rigidity in the back seat by being friendly, conversational and commenting on sights along the way. We came upon some Indians who were clearing away underbrush and cutting tall bamboo trees for constructing buildings. I could see that the logs were about the size of the framing material in our own thatched hut. They were using elephants to carry the heavier logs and pile them in a single area, a sight that I'd seen many times since coming to this part of the world. Elephants, with their enormous strength, were

Sign at initial point of Ledo Road. This road was an unprecedented engineering feat that helped to break the blockade of China.

valuable to the local citizenry as beats of burden. I was alarmed by the sight of one of the elephants which appeared to have a frightening physical problem.

"Look at that elephant!" I exclaimed, pointing excitedly, like a school girl, at the massive red appendage hanging from the animal's abdomen. "I think that elephant is eviscerating. It must have been wounded in some way." I was certain that the vascular pendulous material was intestines, and that everything was simply dropping out of the unfortunate beast.

I turned to look at the colonel. A wave of scarlet swept over his face. He stared straight ahead as if frozen. There was no sound from anyone in the jeep. Mitzi turned around and looked at me with those wide brown eyes that said "shut up" as clearly as if she had spoken. It dawned on me with a thud that I was making all that noise over an elephant's penis. I tried to cover my chagrin with some useless prattle. Mitzi saved the situation by turning around and asking the colonel, "Do you think the quality of the boots they sell in Tinsukia is first rate?"

Shopkeeper smoking his hookah. India offered endless unforgettable sights.

The village of Tinsukia was far from the mainstream of Indian history. There were buildings that were permanent and well preserved, but there were many buildings of wattle and daub, unpaved streets with a thick layer of dust, small shops that sold brass pots, bolts of material for saris, and a leather shop where we hoped to purchase boots. I viewed the town of Tinsukia as I would have looked at a place in a motion picture, the setting of life in an obscure village that had no relationship to anything I had known in my lifetime. What were those two squatting Indians doing, one searching through the thick black hair of the other? They were picking out the lice that infested their oily scalps. Was the shoekeeper, sitting in the entrance of his narrow stall, smoking tobacco in his hookah or something more deadening, like

Naga Indians at bazaar. The Nagas were headhunters but signed a treaty to discontinue the practice until the war was over.

marijuana? What were the children doing, hunched over the refuse-filled gutters? Picking out bits of castaway treasure that might have bartering value? I wondered why the droppings from the sacred cows were being swept up before they lost heat from the animal that had just defecated. I learned that the people mixed straw with the dung then formed it into little patties, stuck the patties on a wall to dry, then used them for fuel. Many of the local people were Nagas, as the area was at the foot of the Naga Hills. The 14th Evac. was high in the Naga Hills, foothills of the Patkai Range. The Nagas were headhunters, but they had signed a treaty with the government that they would cease the practice until the Japanese had been defeated.

Tinsukia, although it retained all of its colorful Indian culture, had been touched by the world of tea planters from Scotland and England. The U.S. Army had a depot there where millions of gallons of fuel were stored, fuel to feed the pipelines, two of them, that stretched from Tinsukia to Myitkyina and beyond. Around the village, the lovely tea plantations flourished. The graceful Assamese women picked the leaves and dropped them into large baskets that they carried on their backs. Many of them had infants cradled in a sack which hung around the torso, and the baby could be breast-fed with no interruption in the labor of harvesting the tea.

A few miles to the west, the Brahmaputra River carried the melting snows of the Himalayas down to the Bay of Bengal and just beyond the river those magnificent mountains formed part of nature's boundary of Tibet, helping to isolate it from the rest of the world. The sun retired into the western sky, leaving a ruddy glow over the slopes where the tea plants shimmered in the changing light. The jeep with its four khaki clad occupants appeared like a blemish on the idyllic landscape.

We had purchased our CBI boots, used up another day and continued to hope and dream of the time when we would be finished with our responsibilities in this foreign land. Mitzi was disgusted with me. "An elephant eviscerating!" she laughed. "You knucklehead!"

Chapter 12

Over the Hump to China

E VERYONE AT the 14th Evac. knew I was regularly seeing one of
the commando pilots. The chief nurse kept close tabs on her staff,
and even she would comment on the unique communication system
Red and I had developed, an air to ground signal that was more efficient
than anything that existed between the hospital and the airbase. One
late afternoon, he came roaring in while I was in the mess. Every eye
turned in my direction as the sound of his plane's motors filled the area
and Kismet's shadow swept over the compound. I could feel my face
go hot and red. I was too self-conscious to jump up and run out to
return his wave, but I knew that in a few hours he'd be there in his
clattering old jeep, and we'd be spending the evening at the airbase
Officers' Club where everyone danced, drank, exchanged stories and
put the war out of mind. War was work, hard work, for all of us, long
hours of using up our lives and energy for something we knew we were
expected to do. We always shared the latest rumors with each other,
talked about assignments that might be coming up and hashed over
old stories of bravery and heartbreak that circulated throughout the
theater. Our need for escape and relaxation was satisfied on those nights
at the club where there was nothing to throttle our camaraderie.

That night Red broke the news that he expected to be moved to
China. My spirits plummeted. "Our commander says the squadron is
going to Liangshan. There's a lot going on in China. Our government
feels that civil war may erupt at any time and no one has made any
decisions about our role. We've got to get the Japs out of there first,
but Chiang is so hung up on keeping the Kuomintang in power he won't
release his armies to fight them. I can't say what our involvement might
be, but the Generalissimo (Chiang Kai-shek) will try to get as much
out of Uncle Sam as he can. You can bet on that."

"I have a brother-in-law in Chungking. He's one of the Naval attachés there," I commented.

"How'd you like to go up to Chungking and visit him?" Red asked, as though Chungking were just down the road. "Our trip to Calcutta didn't seem to upset your captain. Maybe she'd let you go to China with me." The idea was thrilling, but the possibility was remote. "I can't just ask for another three day pass and take off into the 'wild blue yonder,' you know. The captain may not have been aware that I was in Calcutta; I don't think anyone told her and she never asked me where I went. The rules about nurses flitting around the theater are pretty rigid, but maybe if I say I want to visit a relative, she'll let me go. That might be a legitimate reason for travel."

I was stirred up inside with the expectation that I might get into China, to the primitive inland country where so many of my patients had come from. I wanted to see the Hump, those treacherous mountains that reached further into the sky than any place on earth. I wanted to be near Red where I could sort out the configurations of my feelings about him, for no matter where my attention was directed, it always came back to focus on him. Dreaming of such an adventure was dangerous because the dream could so easily be shattered.

I went to our chief nurse, Captain Williams. She was an older woman, homely as a hat full of frogs, but with a motherly sort of heart. Looking back, I think she felt particularly responsible for a few of us because we were so young, so newly out of nursing school, and so vulnerable to certain rapacious military men. I sensed in her a protective attitude toward me, but I was also a little fearful of her, intimidated by her vast experience in a profession where I was but a novice, and by her age and rank, both well beyond my own.

She sat at her desk and eyed me curiously as I walked up to her. "Yes, Lieutenant, what can I do for you?"

"I would like permission to go to China." Her eyes widened and she looked at me with a peculiar smile playing around her mouth. "You have a fever, Lieutenant," she said, with a flat voice, as though she were talking about a patient's symptoms.

"Oh, no Captain. I had a touch of dysentery a few weeks ago, but I've never had a fever." I wondered if she thought I looked ill.

"Young lady, you have a fever for that fly boy!" She said it with all the inflections of a monstrous accusation.

I felt my face burn and my sweaty body squirm inside my cling-
ing bush clothes. Was it so obvious that I was developing a crush on
the young pilot who was buzzing the hospital with his plane? How
could I be so dumb as to think other people didn't notice when Kismet
came skimming the tree tops? My mouth dropped open when I tried
to think of something sensible to say, something that would make her
realize the urgency of going to China, but I could tell by the look on
her face, she had no intention of letting me out of the compound.

"I have a brother-in-law in Chungking. I'd like to visit him," I
said sheepishly.

"The rules are, Lieutenant, that no one flies without orders. It
would be nice if you could go up into China and visit your brother-
in-law, but I cannot let you go. There was a serious plane crash in the
theater only last year, a terrible accident that should never have happened. It involved nurses and Red Cross girls who went over to Chabua
to a party, the plane crashed at Ledo and eighteen lives were lost. The
theater commander really got tough about nurses flying after that."

"Thank you, Captain." I turned and hurried back to my *basha*
before she caught me with tears all over my face. Plunking myself into
a chair, I sat there and cried, not just because she had denied me something that I wanted so much, but because the accumulation of everything had finally pinned me against the wall. The wretched climate,
the food, the longing for home, and now the thought that Red was leaving, seemed too much to bear.

Moments of despair came to all of us, once in a while, and this
one had come to me when no one was around to help me climb over
the mountain of anguish. I wished that Mitzi were there, but she had
been working in the ward where our American patients were and
wouldn't be home for a few more hours. While I sat there, feeling
like an abandoned child, an enormous rat crouched near the burlap
wall watching to see whether or not I was going to move. I sat motionless and watched as he scurried over to the table near where I sat,
climbed the leg of the table and picked up a piece of a cookie that
Mitzi had left there. That brazen rodent was not more than three
feet from me, his beady eyes glistening like buttons, his fur an ugly
mixture of brown and black, his furtive movements accomplishing
his stealthy mission as though he owned the place. Well, he could
have it, I thought.

Living in this dump with all these rats wasn't something I had bargained for. Was I sliding over the edge? Some of the girls did get a little off center but I wasn't about to let that happen to me. I picked up my pen and began to write letters home. My home and family had taken on a new dimension of importance now that we were separated by thousands of miles of ocean, and months and months of not seeing each other. Letters from home were treasures whose value the writer never knew, but the letters that came my way were few and far between because the late summer is one of the busiest on the farm.

The captain hadn't related the tragedy of the plane crash as I had heard it from one of the medical officers. He said that during the holiday season of the previous year a party was held for servicemen in Chabua, the air transport command headquarters. They gathered as many women as they could spare from the hospitals in the Ledo area and flew them over to Chabua for the festivities. Apparently, everyone had too much to drink, which was not uncommon, and by the time they returned to Ledo the field was as fogged in as the revelers were. The pilot missed the field on the first pass, pulled up to circle around and try again, but slammed into the mountain that rose just east of the landing strip. Eighteen lives were lost, most of them female officers. One of the nurses who had driven home from Chabua in a jeep was so devastated by the loss of all her friends that she took her own life. After that, policies concerning nurses' flying about in the theater became much more restrictive than they had been. I was certain that after Red left, I would never get away from the grinding boredom of life at the 14th Evac. I was becoming disturbed by what I saw happening to some of the men and women around me: one nurse was shacked up with the commanding officer of the Ledo airbase; some of the personnel drank excessively; some of the doctors had become disinterested in the sick Chinese patients, and a go-to-hell attitude seemed to permeate the whole atmosphere.

The following day, Red drove to the hospital in the middle of the day. When he found our *basha* empty, he walked over to the ward where I was working. He had never come in the daytime, so I knew something was up. "I have to fly into China tomorrow, up to Liangshan where we'll be moving soon. I'll be flying some equipment up there for our base. Coming with me? We can stop in Chungking and see that relative of yours."

"The captain said I couldn't go. I asked her yesterday," I sulked.

"Let's go ask again," he urged. "She's pretty lenient in most circumstances. Maybe I can soften her up." Red sounded more optimistic than I dared to be. That was another quality in him that I loved—he didn't give up easily and he was quite willing to extend himself in my behalf.

When he approached her, she was very affable. Red explained to her that he'd soon be moving and he'd miss all the folks at the 14th Evac. He buttered her up so well that she didn't even realize how completely she had changed her mind.

"Do you mean we're not going to hear that old plane of yours tearing in at sundown?" she asked. "We'll miss that too."

I could tell he had softened her resolve to keep me out of the air, and she appeared to harbor the same motherly concerns for him as she did for me.

"Lieutenant," she turned to me and said, "I can give you a three day pass. What you do away from the base is your own business and where you go is no concern of mine. If I needed you for nursing service in the ward, I wouldn't let you go, but there's plenty of staff here. Our census is going down every day."

I wanted to jump over the desk to kiss her. The old girl was handing me an adventure that still thrills me when I think about it. "Thank you," I exploded, as she handed me the pass, signed and dated. She had not given me permission to go to China; she had given me certified leave to be away from my station. That's all I needed. Red, too, expressed his appreciation to her. She looked at him and with genuine concern in her voice said, "You damn well get her back here in one piece."

My willingness to soar off into China was another symptom of the relaxation of military rigidity that prevailed. Everyone felt that the war was coming to some kind of conclusion here in India and Burma, conditions in the theater were wretched. We didn't think what we were doing was vital to the cause of winning the war, and we felt that dealing with the Chinese was a hopeless effort. I suppose I could have been court martialed for leaving India, but it never entered my mind. The pass that the chief nurse had given me allowed me to rationalize enough to assuage any guilt I might have felt.

We flew out of Ledo in the early morning, over the Patkai Range that separates India from Burma, over the wide green valley of the Irrawaddy that splits Burma in two. In the next range of mountains the summits were higher and more forbidding than the first. The eastern end of the great Himalaya Range bends sharply southward in that part of Burma and Yunnan Province in China. Great jagged peaks, wearing mists like gauze shrouds were all we could see for a long time. It didn't even occur to me that this was the most dangerous air route on earth; I felt as secure with Red as if I'd been on the train going from home to New York. I sensed, however, that Red and his crew were more alert and tense on this flight than they had been when we flew to Calcutta.

Red talked again of the men in his squadron who had lost their lives on these uncharted elevations. If weather permitted, the pilots could wind their way in and out of the peaks, but the cloud cover was almost always there, adding peril to their many missions. On the first flight that his squadron had made from Myitkyina to Kunming, two planes never returned. There was no way of knowing what happened to the aircraft or their crews, but six months after their disappearance, on a rare day when weather was clear and visibility improved, one of the pilots spotted the wreckage of a plane. On close inspection, he could see that the plane had burned, all except the tail that bore the squadron marking and plane number. Shortly thereafter, the other C-47 was seen and appeared to have suffered the same fate. If either plane had been fifty feet higher, or fifty feet to the right or left, it would have slipped between the peaks, but those evil clouds had been like a web to entrap the innocent airmen. There were so many planes lost flying the Hump that someone had referred to the route as the "aluminum highway."

We saw the Salween River, winding like a silver thread to the Andaman Sea, and nearby the Mekong ran parallel to it, until an eastward turn carried its waters far away through Indo-China and into the South China Sea. The formidable terrain made me shudder, but in the cockpit everything seemed safe and cozy. Red was giving me instructions on all the gadgets and gauges on the dashboard. My attention was directed more to his person than to all the things he was teaching me about flying. I loved the blondness of his lashes as he squinted his eyes to look into the distance. I liked the soft evenness of his voice when he talked to his crew. All the men in the plane, close-knit and compatible, respected him and trusted his judgment. They may have lifted their eyebrows at his smuggling a female officer on board, but they were mute about it. The copilot was very willing to let me sit in his seat, until it was time to land.

"Breakfast in Kunming," Red announced. "The Chinks make good 'ek-us' here." Eggs sounded good to me as we had all missed breakfast because of our early departure from Ledo.

Kunming was a vital point in the airlift to China. It was the first stop for most air travel over the Hump, and the previous year, when the Japanese held the initiative in East China, there had been a great worry as to whether or not the enemy would proceed from the Kweilin-Liuchow-Nanning area and take Kunming. Had they been able to do that, they would surely have swept on to Chungking where the government of the Nationalist Chinese had fled many years before. That threat no longer existed, but the airfield was still a very busy place, where tons and tons of supplies were brought in for Chiang Kai-shek's armies. We ate heartily of the breakfast prepared by the Chinese cooks in an American equipped kitchen, put on a plate which was passed through a little slot in the wall.

Probably, like many other young women my age, I had always associated China with gentle manners, quiet elegance, silk and lacquer. The hallmark of life there was poverty and squalor on a scale difficult for me to comprehend. The oppression, deprivation, and despair in the peasant population was exacerbated by the war, but the war was not an excuse for these conditions, for they had existed for centuries. The people who ruled China, Chiang Kai-shek in particular, were not as greatly concerned with the Japanese invaders as they were with the Chinese Communists who were flexing their muscles in behalf of the enormous number of long-suffering peasants. If the armies of this political faction could wrest power from Chiang, they would no longer be forced to tolerate the warlords or the generals who saved the nation's riches for themselves at the expense of the underlings. It was not until many years later that I became familiar with the complexities of the war in the CBI. History has confirmed that all the exertion of our military forces to enhance the power of the Nationalist Chinese was in vain. We, together with the Chinese, British, Indians and the various hill people of Burma—Chins, Karens and Kachins—succeeded in crushing the Japanese, which, of course was our primary reason for

Red (Arthur Camp) and author in Kunming, the first stop for all planes over the Hump.

being there. Chiang was much more interested in building his Kuomintang army for the war he saw coming, the conflict with the Communist forces.

The flight from Kunming to Chungking was not over such intimidating terrain as the flight from Ledo to Kunming had been, though there were plenty of mountains and miles of rugged land. There were also terraced fields, numberless little walled villages threaded together by dirt roads and footpaths. Aside from oxen-driven carts, wagons pulled by mules, and farmers pushing or pulling their little two-wheeled vehicles, we saw very little motorized traffic. We landed at Chunglung Po Airport in Chungking and the crew put up the ramp at the cargo bay door for the jeep to be brought out. All the crew, along with Red and me, piled in and drove into the city.

Chungking, the wartime capital of China, was a seething city of narrow alleys, steep flights of steps, cliffs honeycombed with caves, the stench of human excreta, heat and filth, gathered beneath an incessant whine of a sing-song Chinese chant and the monotone of tinkling bells. Most of the buildings looked like tier upon tier of dirty unpainted structures closing in the airless streets in a claustrophobic scene of war-time improvisation. Automobiles, jeeps, a few trucks, and other vehicles of both the American and Chinese authorities were winding up and down the narrow, dirty streets, but most of the motion was the rickety wheels of little carts being pulled by Chinese coolies, the hundreds of shabby pedestrians that padded along noiselessly, rickshaws and palanquins, and soldiers, the very kind that had come to our Assam jungle hospital for medical attention. At that time, the term "culture-shock" had not been used, but for me, that first view of Chungking was a staggering blow to my sensibilities.

In the late afternoon, we went to the Office of the Naval Command where we hoped to see my brother-in-law, but he had been sent on a mission somewhere down river toward Shanghai, and would be gone for weeks. The commander treated us as though we were visiting dignitaries and offered us the use of a command car so that we could drive through Chungking unmolested, that is, we wouldn't have to worry about being stopped by military police. Our plane's crew could keep the jeep for their own convenience, and Red and I could investigate this war-time capital of China by ourselves.

The first imperative, then, was to find a place where I could spend the night. If I went to an army installation, it was possible that I would be asked to state my mission, since I was wearing the uniform of the Army Nurse Corps, indicating dignity of purpose. I couldn't say that I was on a lark, visiting a relative, or gathering memories for my future grandchildren. The matter of finding a place to spend the night was a prickly little concern, for in that era, nice girls just did not sleep around. Sex, outside the boundaries of marriage, was considered cheap and licentious, and I was not about to bed down with this guy who appealed to me so much, and he, fortunately, didn't suggest anything other than finding suitable billeting for me. Our relationship was warm and sweet; I didn't want it to develop into a hot, steamy romance running out of control. Most of the nurses, like myself, were concerned for our reputations within our professional community. We did not want the stigma of a "horizontal Harriet" or to be marked as an indiscreet philanderer. To my friends and colleagues, flying off to China alone with Red created appearances that I hoped would not be misconstrued. My innate caution and wariness served me well in a world of sensual feeling where it might have been easy to abandon virtuous conduct. Red's tender kiss set my heart aquiver, and when he enfolded me in his arms, I was very aware of his passion, as a man cannot so easily conceal desire as a woman can. Perhaps, if it had been more convenient, we would have succumbed to our biological yearnings, but always, in the recesses of my mind, was the vision of my mother, her jaw set and her eyes narrowed and piercing as she burned into my being the words, "You make your bed, and you'll sleep in it." Because the word "sex" was poisonous to her, she never formulated that threat into appropriate words, but I knew what she meant. Even though I was acutely aware of the hormonal messages that bombarded me, a rigid Presbyterian background held me fast to the mores of my upbringing.

We decided to check out the Red Cross and see if they had billeting for army personnel. I walked into their headquarters and was offered a room, no questions asked.

The room was barren and bleak, but then beggars are not choosers. In my musette bag, I carried pajamas and personal grooming items and extra khakis, stiff with rice starch. They were accordion pleated by the time I unfolded them for wearing. At the end of a long corridor was an Army-type latrine, but I found no water for washing my face. There were no other people around, everything was hollow and silent, as though the building had been recently evacuated. I put on my night clothes and climbed onto the mattress, a cotton sack filled with straw. I didn't mind that, after all, I was by this time accustomed to the dearth of physical comforts in the Far East. The straw crackled when I settled into it and sought a restful position. No sooner had I found just the right spot and prepared to drift off into blissful slumber when the first biting insect tasted my warm blood. Before I knew it, the fleas were eating me alive. There was no possibility of sleeping in the middle of such infestation, so I got up and put my clothes back on, and dragged the paillasse off the bed to the floor. Then I lay, fully clothed, on the boards that had held the flea-infested straw bedding. I don't know where the crew slept that night, but wherever it was, it could not have been less comfortable than my den of fleas.

In the morning, Red came for me in the command car that had been offered to us by the Naval attaché. We set out to see this city, perched on a cliff over the confluence of the Chialing and the Yangtze rivers. The cliffs were defaced with boarded up caves where the people had once tried to flee the cruelty of Japanese civilian bombing raids. There was a fair amount of traffic on the muddy rivers—some flat bottom scows that transported rice from the rich farm land of Szechwan, honey-barges that carried the human waste used for fertilizer, and other small boats whose business was not readily apparent.

The people we saw looked frail and fatigued, and they barely glanced in our direction. So many people carried heavy burdens on their backs or at the ends of poles slung across their backs, that they were indeed a weighted down society. Men who carried the ubiquitous shoulder pole developed a pad of thick, crusty skin where the pole rested. I saw none of that spontaneous gaiety that was in the Chinese soldiers, none of that laughter floated on the surface of their mean and comfortless lives. Many, in fact most, of the people in Chungking were refugees, pushed far into the interior of China to escape being servile to the Japanese. Some of them had come from coastal cities where they had been used to far better living conditions. Everything that I saw with my eyes, I perceived simultaneously with my nose, and so my view was tainted by the awful smells that exuded from dark, narrow, smoky alleys. There was no escape from the stink that attacked our nostrils at every turn. A thin fog hovered around the city; the moisture undoubtedly made the smells more pungent. Permanently imprinted in my memory is an old woman I saw that day. She sat solemnly on the bottom step of a steeply rising rickety stairway. In the deep sag of the filthy trousers that formed her lap, she cradled a brightly feathered chicken. As she rocked back and forth, a weak, grunting sound came from her toothless mouth, as though she were urging the chicken to bring forth an egg. And it did! The old lady picked the egg from her lap, put it in her pocket and walked away. The chicken was tethered with a piece of twine and followed after her as she walked off with her treasure, possibly a meal that she would share with another.

The Americans in China lived totally insulated from the Chinese on the streets and in the byways. Government buildings and hotels were all taken over by the Nationalist government and the Americans. Chang Kai-shek was squeezing so much out of the United States that he was careful not to offend Americans by expecting them to lower their standard of living while in his country. He and his Wellesley educated wife understood American ways and ideas, but they were far removed from the reality of their own peoples' lives. Red and I ate a splendid dinner, better than we had had in months, at an Officers' Club in Chungking.

We were sorry not to have seen my sister's husband, Bill. He told us later of his trip down the river, traveling sometimes on water and other times in an army vehicle on a road through the banks of loess, a yellowish kind of loam deposited by wind and water. Among other strange happenings, I remember his account of a meal he ate along the way. Food, in the countryside of China, was not abundant. There seemed never enough for everyone to have an adequate diet. He and a few army people stopped in a village to eat. They were served a delicious meal of meat and vegetables on steaming rice, a repast that satisfied the hunger that had built up over the long, uncomfortable ride in a weapon's carrier. Upon leaving the place where they had eaten, Bill observed a wall where many rat skins had been stretched out and pinned to dry. He also saw a half-dozen big rats tied by their long tails, hanging and squirming violently in a futile effort to free themselves. He wondered if they were the next meal to be served, and he speculated, too, as to what kind of meat he had just enjoyed so much. In China it was best to enjoy whatever was served and not ask questions.

By the time we were ready to return to our Indian bases, I had soaked up so much of the reality of China that I had trouble digesting all that I saw. It was easier now for me to understand the Chinese patients' behavior and their willingness to accept sickness and death as the ordinary circumstances of life. If I had little comprehension of the tangled events of the China-Burma-India campaign, they knew nothing beyond the fact that they followed blindly the dictates of their superior officers and were fortunate to have their *chá and fàn.*

Our time was limited for we had to hurry on to Liangshan, a considerable distance beyond Chungking. We wasted no time accomplishing Red's mission as we hoped to return over the highest mountains before darkness fell. It would be very late by the time we arrived in our home territory.

The long flight home gave Red and me hours to visit and talk about what we had seen and done in the theater. On one of his missions to drop rice and supplies to a group of Burmese hill soldiers who had just won a victory over the Japs, he landed Kismet in a rice paddy. The field was covered with dead Japanese and the victorious Kachins were celebrating. They had a captured soldier whom they had interrogated, not just with words, but apparently with rifle butts. After Red and his crew had off-loaded the provisions, they asked him to take the Japanese soldier with him and push him out when the plane was high in the air.

"You didn't, of course?" I asked, thinking of how the Chinese could so easily cast one of their own out of a plane.

"Good Lord, no," he answered, "haven't you heard of 'war crimes?' And anyway, I could never do a thing like that even though I hate those damn Japs." Red told me about their squadron's flights to Meiktila, down below Mandalay. The major battles of the war in the CBI, conflicts that involved American servicemen, had been in Burma and most of our activity was related in one way or another to the fierce warfare that had taken place to drive the Japanese out of that country. The British had inched their way through Central Burma, crossed the Irrawaddy and captured Meiktila, splitting the Japanese forces, leaving some of the enemy to the north of Meiktila, severed from their lines of supply. Many of the enemy tried to escape to the south but were defeated by the treachery of the terrain and the lack of food. The British army had several Indian divisions fighting in Burma, as well as some Chinese. The 317th Troop Carrier Squadron transported these troops, their ammunition, food and supplies to Meiktila.

"We lost one of our planes in Meiktila," Red told me. "A mortar shell exploded under the plane and broke it in two. And another of our pilots found his plane riddled with bullet holes when he got back to Ledo. The fighting there was pretty intense."

"Were the Japs still there when you were airlifting supplies?" I asked.

"You bet they were. Sometimes we had to circle the airfield for a long time before we could bring the plane in. We had to wait for the British to recapture the field. The Japs would all run to the perimeter of the landing strip and shoot at us as we came in. One time an older fellow was with me—he'd been in the Pacific campaign and seen a lot of action—when the Japs began lobbing mortar shells onto the field. It sounded like a 4th of July celebration to me, but not to him. He grabbed my arm and said, 'Let's get the hell out of here,' when my inclination was to hang around to see what was happening."

"Isn't Meiktila the place where our OSS men found out how the Japanese camouflaged their aircraft?" I questioned.

"Yeh, they captured a Jap pilot and he had a photograph of himself standing by his Zero. Our intelligence saw these holes in the picture, black spots in the field. What they were looking at was dug out areas where the planes could be stored, and on the top the Japs had put sod, so that from the air it looked like an ordinary rice paddy."

"Clever, aren't they?" I commented.

"Our bombers went into Meiktila then and bombed the hell out of the place. That sure cut back on the number of aircraft the Japs had to work with. This was earlier. The British began a drive toward Rangoon after Meiktila, as they wanted to push northward from Rangoon and squeeze the Japs from both directions."

"Well, it worked, didn't it?" I commented.

"I guess the next thing we have to think about is what our role will be in China. There's much talk about a blockade of Japan, but now that we've taken Okinawa it won't be necessary to invade southeast China and get back our airbases there."

"How much longer do you expect this war to go on?" I asked, always feeling that men were omniscient about such things.

"Depends on the enemy now. Either they surrender or we invade their homeland. No one knows just how we'll win this war, but we'll win, and that's a certainty."

At the Yalta conference in February of 1945, the Allies thought that after Germany's defeat, the war with Japan might go on for about eighteen months. Victory in Europe had been achieved and the focus of the war was now in the Far East. It was late summer. The strategists were talking about a direct invasion of Japan with the possibility of a million American casualties.

We stopped again in Kunming to refuel before heading home. As Kismet gained altitude, the green terraced rice fields of the high plateau where the city sits fell away. The violet blue waters of Lake Tien Chih stretched like an inland sea far to the south of the city. We climbed to the top of the surrounding mountains whose desolate tops appeared to reach up to touch the plane's belly, seemingly only inches away from the sharp, gray rock pinnacles of the Hump. The C-47s could not fly much higher than twelve or thirteen thousand feet, so most of the time we were skimming close enough to scrape the paint. Red said it was one of those rare times when the hovering mists were not there to obscure the very tops of the mountains. Those jagged, rocky elevations looked cold and inhospitable, a place where you would never want to find yourself. Soon Red dropped his plane into the green Irrawaddy Valley, soared over the ridges that separate Burma from India, and let down to treetop level. There was an exhilarating sense of deliverance to hear the landing gear coming down as we approached the home base at Ledo.

It was late when I crept into my little straw house, but I had no feeling of fatigue, only a joyful sensation of having soared into a wild new world of ardor and adventure. I lay in the warm, sticky capsule of tropical air under the mosquito netting thinking about the future. What would I do when the war was over? Make a career of the military? Go back to school? There was no doubt in my mind that I could do anything I wanted to do once I got back to the States. I tried not to think of whether the ginger-haired pilot who had just flown me back from China would have any place in my life. This was not a time to make big decisions. When I returned to the equilibrium of normal living, when the peace was established, when I was at last in my familiar environment—that was the time to mark out a diagram of the upcoming years and plan for the future.

I was beginning to feel that my nursing skills were getting stale, that my experience with tropical diseases was the only thing I had added to my knowledge. This worried me. I hoped fervently that I would soon be assigned to a general hospital where I could practice good techniques and renew my self confidence. However, traveling in these Oriental lands was an enrichment that I hadn't counted on, and thanks to Red, who was offering me a front row seat, I was seeing far more of the world than my cohorts stuck back in the jungle.

Every American who served his country during the war had a different experience, ranging from withering boredom to excruciating terror. No matter where he fought, whether on the battlefields of Europe, in the skies over the Hump, or in the islands of the Pacific, the common denominator was loneliness and longing for home. From general to GI, the ache to return home was a merciless gnawing at the periphery of our young souls. We all felt that we were in limbo, moving about in a world where the normal rhythm of life had been interrupted. Innocently, we believed that we would return to the paths we were traversing when war came upon us, but nothing would be the same again—ever. America was a different nation and the youth who took off the uniforms of service never peeled off the hubris that went with them.

There was no combat activity in the theater now, but neither had there been a surrender. We were worn out with expectancy, hoping to hear that the hospital would close—there were fewer and fewer patients—that we might get a new assignment, that some of us might even go home. Red would soon leave for Liangshan and my world would change, that was certain.

In the meantime the weather in Assam was improving, the heat had dissipated and the rains had subsided. The 14th Evac. and its personnel, the doctors and nurses who had rendered lifesaving services to sick and wounded soldiers, was a sluggish, spiritless institution.

Chapter 13

A Visit from a Jungle Beast

R ED'S SQUADRON, while they waited to move to China, continued to make drops of food and supplies to the OSS troops still in Northern Burma. Sometimes they were able to fly into a rice paddy or a cleared area and deliver their cargo rather than drop it by parachute now that the Japanese had retreated to their bases in eastern China. He flew over to Dinjan one day and picked up a shipment of fresh meat to carry out to the units who were deep in the jungle. When a ship came into the docks at Calcutta, there was frequently special cargo for men in the forward areas, frozen meat being one commodity treasured by the Americans. This beef, packed in boxes, had been rushed up to the ATC base, broken down into various amounts to be distributed to units all around the Assam and North Burma area. For some reason, the medical units were rarely on the list to receive this luxury. We never saw fresh meat in our mess in all the months that I was at the 14th Evac. Red must have remembered how bitterly I complained about the food because, after his mission to deliver the meat, he drove up to the hospital with one of those boxes in his jeep. The box contained about a half dozen steaks, the best that our own western ranches produced. A group of us, including Mitzi and Tom, gathered in the back of our *basha* to fill our empty stomachs with this rare treat.

It had been a spectacularly beautiful night. The brilliant Indian moon silhouetted the thatched roof buildings and the tall spindly bamboos. Our faces, vividly yellowed from atabrine, reflected the resplendent scene. We held the meat on sticks and cooked it over a little fire, licked our fingers and talked of our backyard cook-outs back home. The air in those far away hills was pure and clear; the moon and stars seemed nearer and brighter, the heavens darker and deeper than anywhere on earth.

Author at back door of our basha. These structures had a brief life. Ours was deteriorating fast.

"Thanks ol' chap," Tom said to Red as he got ready to leave. "That's the first bit of beef I've had since coming to the remount camp. That was like being at my own table in Yorkshire which I've not seen in five years. I'm hungry for old Blighty, I am."

"Won't be long now," Red said, "we've got the Japs on the run. There's no more Zeros in the sky, and I've heard their navy has been decimated. I just wish Tojo would surrender before Uncle Sam decides to invade their islands."

"You're the only country left with the resources to do that," Tom added. "You'd have to count the Brits out on that one."

We said good-bye to Tom. He and Mitzi walked out to his jeep, then Red and I said our tender goodnights.

Our little *basha* sat close to the edge of a stream, a raging torrent after a monsoon rain, or a deep rocky gulch when the weather was dry. On the other side of this water, the jungle was an impenetrable thickness of tall trees and shorter banana plants, bushes, vines, and other tangled undergrowth. We could see orchids growing high in the branches, but we never entered that formidable barrier of trees because it was full of insects, snakes, and leeches. Monkeys lived there happily chattering and jumping through the twisting vines, waking us in the morning with their shrill, scolding voices. After our cook-out, I took the box that the meat had been in to the edge of the stream, away from the *basha*, so that flies would not seek out the blood that remained on the bottom of the box.

That night, full and blissful, I got ready for bed with the nightly ritual of getting the mosquito netting arranged just right. I tucked it securely under the cot's thin mattress, leaving a small opening to crawl under, then when I was inside I pushed the remaining segment of netting as far under my body as I could reach. The mosquitoes did not intimidate me the way the rats did, and the mosquito control unit worked hard to keep these insects away from the hospital area. I knew that mosquito netting was no protection from rats, but somehow, I always felt better when the netting was securely in place. One of the nurses had awakened one morning and found a rat in bed with her, a reminder that rats, considering their numbers and their brazen behavior, might climb onto the cot while I slept.

I lay in the cocoon-like enclosure that the mosquito netting created, my head resting in the bend of my arm where I wore a watch with a luminous dial. It was exactly midnight. I thought, "Another day gone; another day closer to home." Sleep came quickly, as it does in the young.

Suddenly, I was awake, aware of another presence in the room. Something with warm breath was pushing the mosquito netting into my face. The deep, low, throaty rumble of an animal was coming from the same place as the breath, coming directly into my face. I smelled the wildness, the unfamiliar odor of an animal's mouth. Except for the thin film of netting, there was nothing between my face and whatever intruder had wandered through the opening to the *basha*. He continued to push the netting all up and down my body, as though smelling. I lay paralyzed with fear, for I quickly decided that this beast was a tiger. I remembered the stories that were told of men working on the Ledo Road being attacked by tigers, viciously mauled, then brought to the hospital. I could see the distinct outline of the animal in the moonlight that filtered into the little bamboo house, and the size of the image reinforced my belief that this was indeed a tiger. I thought my heart would rupture my chest with its violent pounding. I tried to breathe noiselessly, but every inspiration and every expiration sounded like a rasping bellows. I wanted to call out to Mitzi on the other side of the bamboo partition, but my mouth was bone dry, and the terror in my heart had turned my tongue to concrete. I feared that any sound, any movement, would precipitate an attack. I knew that I was going to die; there was no escape from this beast who was so close that I could feel his fur. Death was so upon me that I seemed to be outside myself, watching the drama unfold as though I were a spectator and not a participant. I visualized this beast sinking his long, sharp teeth into me, pulling me off the cot and into the jungle. My parents would be horrified to learn that I'd been eaten by a tiger. Maybe no one would ever know what happened. Fear, unspeakable fear, coagulated in my thumping heart, but I knew instinctively that I must stay as motionless as possible. While I lay there, I began to wonder if this was a nightmare. Was I dreaming? Over and over I mentally oriented myself to the situation, and then the animal seemed to have left the room. I hoped that some noise in the compound would alert the animal and that he'd run off, but the area was very still.

Only the intermittent hum and chirr of night insects drifted into our *basha*. My muscles began to ache from holding such a rigid position, but when I tried to relax, they trembled, causing the cot to shake. When the cot moved, I saw the beast again. He had leaped up onto the shelf where my clothing was stored and he raised his head at the small sound that the cot had made. I was choking to death with fear. Was he resting up there, standing guard over his next meal? The anxiety of imminent death, I decided, was more unbearable than death itself. I began to hope the beast would attack and get the whole thing over with, but he lay stretched out on the shelf, ready to pounce if I moved. For hours, I was a prisoner of a wild beast, an animal that had no doubt come to the edge of the clearing, over the little stream, where the scent of fresh meat from that bloody box had lured him. Dawn came and I was able to get a clearer view of my captor, and I knew, at last, that he was not a tiger. He was black, jet black, with fur that had a magnificent sheen and glimmered with swirls like wavy "cow-licks." He was not as massive as a tiger, but his long black body stretched out behind a sleek head with wide set narrowed yellow eyes, was every bit as lethal as any cat that inhabits this part of the world. As the morning light increased, he jumped silently from his perch and walked out between the two limp curtains that we called a door. I started to cry, then went in to tell Mitzi about our nocturnal visitor. She was unaware of the heart-stopping drama that had taken place on the other side of the bamboo partition. I called for the guard, but I don't think he believed me—at first. Then Corbi, our bearer, came and he in turn called another native man who said the marks in the dirt were the prints of a leopard. He told us that there had been a black leopard in the area for some time, and it had been seen by many of the local Nagas. I wrote a letter home to tell my parents about this grisly experience, and to my dismay, they had the letter printed in the local newspaper.

Mitzi and I requested that a door be put on the entrance, so someone responsible for the buildings in the compound had a panel of woven split bamboo placed over the opening and a latch attached so that we would close the door when we went to bed. That was a comfort, but never again did I crawl under that mosquito netting without a sickening twinge of fear. It was not until we moved out of the 14th Evac. that I slept with a sense of security.

When I reported to my ward for duty I felt exhausted. It wasn't easy to concentrate on the duties that lay before me, but somehow strength came and being busy made the hours go by quickly. As I was leaving the mess at noon, Captain Williams came up to me and asked, "Are you okay, Lieutenant? I heard that you had a rough night. You may go to your *basha* now and get some sleep and I'll find someone to cover your ward."

I was never so grateful for anything. The fatigue that overtook me was like a malignancy, all consuming and total. The men who fought in the jungles suffered from this kind of fatigue, brought on by fear of the enemy that lurked behind every tree and every rise in the terrain. This kind of exhaustion, added to their physical exertion, sapped their vitality and left them with a kind of tiredness that lingered for weeks. It was a very long time before I felt like myself again.

Some of the men began talking of experiences they had had with the wild beasts that were abundant in the surrounding jungles. One of the engineers who worked on the construction of the Ledo Road told me that he had entered his tent one night and found a Bengal tiger sitting in the middle of it. He turned and fled, falling into a deep irrigation ditch that enclosed the area. The tiger, in its eagerness to leave, leapt over him as he crouched in the ditch. Mitzi and Tom had seen a tiger cross the road as they traveled one day toward the Pangsau Pass. There were many snakes in the reports of animal sightings, but I never saw one.

We began working shorter shifts, for the patient load was diminishing rapidly. I was sorry to have less time to spend on the wards, because there was nothing to do if you were not on duty. The Chinese soldiers came to regard the nurses as strong allies and friends. They thought we were omniscient, that in our own country we were powerful and glorified human beings. Their concept of democracy was nebulous and poorly understood. They believed that in every country there were a handful of men with wealth and power and millions of men like themselves who were subservient to them, and this they accepted without questioning. They called me "number one Lieutenant" or "Missy Lieutenant." They looked forward to the mornings when I made rounds and asked how they were getting on, each soldier a peasant with his own set of concerns. I could see, as I approached their *chwángs*, they were preparing for the encounter. Sometimes it was just a new English word that the soldier had learned, a word he was eager to spring on me as a surprise, or a comment about the C-47 that they thought was going to crash into the hospital as it roared down through the tree tops. Even they knew the pilot was my friend, and they laughed in a teasing way to let me know they were aware that he had his eye on me.

One day, one of the sick men beckoned me to his *chwáng*. He reached into his little bag of pathetic personal belongings and brought forth a worn photo. "*Chi-dz*," he spoke with a soft voice as he handed me the picture of a delicately beautiful Oriental girl.

"*Jya dua chi-dz?*" I asked. My Chinese was not good, but I was attempting to ask if he was going home to his wife.

"Japanese" was the only word I understood in the answer he gave me, but from the sorrowful look that settled over his face I guessed that she had been a victim of the plunder of his homeland.

It was near this time that we heard the news that a bomb had been dropped on Japan, a bomb of such devastating power that it would end the war. Since I knew nothing about the development of an atomic bomb, that report, at first, did not make a big impression. We had become accustomed to hearing about cities being destroyed by "saturation bombing." The world seemed weary of bombing, so what was different about this monstrous bomb that was dropped on Hiroshima? Then news came to us that Nagasaki had been wiped from the face of Japan by a single bomb. We all knew, deep in our bones that the war was finished, but we held back our euphoria until the official Japanese surrender on August 14, 1945. Even the expressions on the faces of the hospital personnel we passed on the little footpaths changed. A new vitality erupted, a meaningful bustle to get things done. There developed a great urgency to empty the hospital beds and make plans for closing the 14th Evac. I had learned that the wheels of the military grind at a maddeningly slow pace, so it was no surprise that we all hung for weeks in suspended expectancy. Even so, knowing that the war was over gave us all cause to rejoice, each of us holding her dreams closer and visualizing herself on the shores of home. But there was that nagging little question about China: Would Red and his squadron be there for a long time? Would some of the nurses be assigned to hospitals there? Would Uncle Sam continue to support Chiang Kai-shek in his efforts to rid China of the Communists?

Tex came to my *basha* to invite me to the hospital's Officers' Club to celebrate V-J Day. I knew what that would be like—a huge punch bowl made from the plexiglass bubble of some aircraft, filled with a deadly concoction of every kind of booze available. Many of the men and women would drink too much and by midnight there would be khaki-clad arms and legs everywhere, especially in the drainage ditches that ran along side the narrow, winding pathways in the compound. Staying on the path at night was difficult in a sober state; impossible in a staggering intoxicated state.

"I'm sorry, Tex, but I've already accepted an invitation to the club at the airbase." I could see that he was nettled.

"You've been seeing a lot of that Hot Shot Charlie kid, haven't you? Well, you better make up your mind, it's either me or the fly boy."

I had not been aware that our relationship was such a serious one. He was asking me, in his way, to "knock off" seeing Red, something that I was not inclined to do.

"Red's being transferred to Liangshan soon. I won't be seeing him for a while, if ever."

I could see that this news pleased Tex as his irritation subsided noticeably. Working professionally with him had been a solid pleasure, for he had an innate curiosity about diseases, their etiology, the course they took and what treatments and medications were the most effective. With a large patient population, he was able to apply some of his best ideas, and he explained everything in a way that I found stimulating. He had a certain conceit that I didn't know how to handle, and I knew, intuitively, that as soon as he found out that I was really a hick from the backwoods of Pennsylvania, he would no longer be interested in me. Many people of my generation thought that good looks and intelligence belonged to the Ivy League, that farms produced clumsy hayseeds. All my life I had endured the derision of those more affluent and sophisticated folk.

V-J Day came and went, and all the wild celebrations that we had didn't change things very much. For a brief moment, everyone's morale peaked like a pinnacle of joy in a bleak depression, then things returned to their weary grind. We worked and waited.

Chapter 14

A Surreptitious Flight
to Hsian, China

A RESTLESSNESS OVERTOOK the staff at the hospital. Change was imminent, but we were frustrated with the snail-like pace of that change. Knowing that we would soon be separated from each other, leaving only that warmth that develops among comrades who have endured much hardship together, we seemed to become friendlier and more communicative. We even approached our work with an enthusiasm that had lain dormant beneath our feelings of hopelessness. We had not yet absorbed the reality of victory over the Japanese; for us it meant only one thing—going home! I could not imagine a morning when I would not be entering that long *basha* where dozens of Chinese soldiers waited eagerly for me to give them medicine, dress their wounds, and exchange words and expressions in each other's language that confirmed our human bond. They knew that evacuation from our hospital was certain, but some of them talked openly of fighting against the Communists. Being at war was a way of life for these men, for they had not known peace in their adult years.

Keenly aware that the end of the war would directly impact each one of us, we lived on a diet of rumors, believed wholeheartedly those that we wanted to and rejected as gossip those that sounded distasteful.

I also knew that Red's squadron would be leaving Ledo in a matter of days, so being with him was one of my priorities. He had another assignment to fly into China, this time up to Hsian, and he again invited me to go with him. Fearing that Captain Williams would think I was taking advantage of her good nature if I asked for another pass, I negotiated with one of the other nurses to cover my ward of patients. The

In pilot's seat of Kismet. Red taught me how to read the instrument panel.

census on the ward was considerably reduced and thereby the work-load. I didn't discuss my forthcoming trip, except with Mitzi, as flying around China, like Red and I had done before, would probably not be condoned by the higher military echelon in the theater. We thought it best to be as surreptitious as possible this time, even though the general attitude was quite relaxed and non-restrictive. Nobody was paying much attention to what we were doing as long as we managed to get our work done and report for briefings that were posted in the mess. The war was over in Europe and in the Pacific and now in China. The world was an exhausted, wounded sphere, but China was not yet ready to draw the curtain on the great drama that had swept the land. There was this play within a play that would now take center stage. The civil war that was coming to a boil all those years, while the nation struggled with the Japanese invasion, was about to erupt with renewed savagery.

The city where we were going had historical significance in the rise of power of China's Communist leaders. Chang Hsueh-liang, better known as the Young Marshall—he is now know as Zhang Xueliang, and lives in New York City—commander of the Manchurian troops, had in 1936 kidnapped Chiang Kai-shek in Hsian, an incident that shook the world. He had tried to persuade Chiang to abandon the civil war and form a united front against the Japanese, which the obstinate little general did in a most reluctant way. Strange as it seems, it was the Communist Chou En-lai who insisted upon the release of Chiang, for he realized that the Generalissimo was the one personality that could hold the country together and keep it from sinking to its knees before the Japanese onslaught. Hsian became the headquarters of the Communist armies. As the years went by, their numbers and their strength increased, while the armies of the Kuomintang became weaker and more corrupt. With the Japanese defeated, the world held its breath to see what would happen next in China.

As we had done on that first flight over the Hump to Kunming, then on to Chungking, we stayed overnight in the familiar places of our previous visit, then went on to Hsian. When Red brought Kismet onto the landing strip southwest of the ancient walled city, the crew put up the ramp so the jeep could be unloaded. Before this maneuver was complete, a swarm of people gathered around to watch what we were doing. I suspect that there were hundreds of Chinese there who had never before seen an American, especially an American woman. We gazed at each other in equal wonder. These peasants were working on the airstrip, perhaps enlarging it for future military purposes. The elderly ones were carrying baskets of pebbles that hung from either ends of poles slung over their weary shoulders. The little ones, some appeared to be no more than three and four years old, were placing these pebbles adjacent to each other to form a smooth, flat surface. Just as they had, centuries ago, constructed the Great Wall, these serfs were building an airstrip entirely with their hands. There was no vehicle or machine more sophisticated than a wheelbarrow in sight. There was a sadness that permeated this silent encounter, for I saw the children squinting through a thick exudate of diseased eyes, their frail bodies unwashed, poorly fed. The old ones, leathery and wrinkled from exposure to Hsian's brutal winters and scorching summers, had distrust as well as curiosity in their intense stare. Even so, I was able to discern a quality of gentleness in their faces, as I had seen in the sick Chinese patients. It was not easy to equate these docile people with the popular perception that they have a profound disregard for life, particularly the life of an individual man.

We hopped into the jeep and drove to the gates of the city. Outside the walls that surrounded the airfield, and spread over the countryside, were thousands of blue clad soldiers, *pings*, they were called, encamped in groups. These, we later learned, were Communist soldiers waiting, perhaps to make a move at the propitious moment. There was no doubt that some kind of military action would soon take place here; the whole scene gave off an atmosphere of impending collision. We roared through the gate, a gate set in walls of colossal dimensions, walls that had protected the city for eleven centuries before the birth of Christ. Who would ever have guessed that this filthy, dusty, rundown city had once been the ancient capital of the Han and T'ang dynasties, the starting point of the Silk Road that stretched across Asia from Canton in the East to Alexandria, Egypt, in the West. This was the conduit for silk, jade and spices, but more than that, a route for communication and the exchange of culture and the spread of knowledge. Here, again, the suffocating odors assaulted our noses with a vengeance. Eyes, dark with fatigue and hunger, peered at us from the dust-covered stone streets and the shabby unpainted buildings. Again, I saw children with infected eyes, their thin legs covered with excoriated areas that were probably scratch marks caused by the unrelenting itching of untreated scabs. I believed that the Chinese were a people of an uncomplaining nature, accepting whatever lot befell them, without questioning or resistance. My heart ached to see their forlorn and dispirited faces, their undernourished bodies and the absence of hope for something better. In retrospect, those observations were quite subjective. I now believe that they did have dreams of a better life and that they were certain that Communism was the pathway to it.

The main street of the city was paved with stone blocks, but over them lay a film of brown dust, the same dun colored sediment that covered everything else. The buildings along the street were in disrepair, but like every other place in China that we had seen, out of the doorways, the windows, the chinks and crevices, came the essence of stale urine, smoking cooking oils, spices, offal, wet dogs, and rancid sweat— a potpourri of offensive odors. Neither Red nor I had much desire to linger around Hsian, and since his business was at the airport and not in the city, we hurried on our way. We also hoped to stop in Chungking again to check out whether Bill had returned from his lengthy trip away from the naval station.

Again we were disappointed in not seeing my brother-in-law, but at Chunglung Po Airport we saw a most impressive entourage of long black limousines flying American flags and winding out onto the field. Whoever was riding in that caravan must have had considerable political stature. Our conjecture was that it was General Wedemeyer, Ambassador Patrick Hurley, or even Chiang Kai-shek himself. I began to feel uneasy about being in a place where I had no authorization to be, and had a joyous sense of relief when Kismet lifted off the runway and headed for Assam. When we arrived in Ledo, Red got a jeep and drove me back to the 14th Evac., over the nineteen miles of road where every bump and every curve had become as familiar to us as the country lanes and city streets of our homes in the USA. I didn't know, when he kissed me goodnight, that I would not see him again for a very long time. He and his squadron moved to Liangshan the next day.

There were many rumors about reassignment for the nurses, and in the midst of these I did get reassigned—to the officers' ward where we had a few sick nurses! This was not a back breaking job, since nurses, when they are ill, insist upon caring for themselves, and these girls were motivated to get better in a hurry because the unit was about to be shut down and the personnel reassigned. As fast as evacuation could be accomplished, the Chinese were sent to mustering points where, when seating space was available, they were loaded on planes and flown to receiving stations on the other side of the mountains, and those in better condition were exported in trucks over the Ledo Road, back to their native land.

Yang came looking for me one day. He was tense and uneasy, little beads of sweat trickled over his forehead as I invited him into the nurses' station of the American ward. (The Chinese personnel never, never stepped over the threshold of an American ward.) "For you, Lieutenant," he said as he handed me a slender roll of newsprint. Inside was a handsome pair of ivory chopsticks, engraved in Chinese characters with his name, my name and the date.

"Yang, what a lovely gift!" I was embarrassed by such generosity, for I knew that this young man had neither rupees nor yuan to spare. "*Xie Xie*, (thank you) Yang," I said examining the delicate brush marks in red and black on the proximal end of each chopstick.

"I want you never forget me, Lieutenant. Someday I come to America. We eat rice together on Broadway, okay? You use *kwái-dz* (chopsticks), I use *cha-dz* (fork)." He smiled his most engaging smile. He had been such a valuable adjutant to my nursing responsibilities that without him I would surely have failed miserably. What the patients had to tell me about their symptoms was filtered to me through Yang; what I needed to say to the patients went through Yang in the other direction. Getting a message across to the patient would have been a futile charade had it not been for Yang Pei-jen who built a bridge of confidence between our two languages. This was the first in a long line of farewells that began, even though no military orders had been cut for any of us. Thus began the process of tearing apart a fabric of relationships that made it possible for the Americans to fulfill humanitarian service where one nation of Oriental people had sought to consume another nation of Oriental people.

My clothing was becoming very shabby. That was to be expected as the *dhobis* didn't just launder them in the way that we understood washing clothes. They flogged the very life out of every garment, ridding themselves of many burning hostilities stored in their souls, as they beat the khaki pants and khaki shirts with fury. Woolen uniforms became musty and mildewed because we never wore them and had no place to store them except in the footlocker under the cot. The climate was destructive to everything: shoes broke apart from excessive moisture, flashlight batteries corroded and ceased to work, stationery and envelopes stuck together, rendering them useless. Except for the PX, with its very limited supply of everything, there was no place to buy the necessities that we had always taken for granted. I knew when we got down to Calcutta, if that was our destination, we could purchase a bolt of cotton and the Indian tailors would turn it into perfectly fitting garments in little more than a day. In the meantime, we all learned how to get along with less, to improvise, and to share with each other the things that we had. Occasionally one of the nurses would get a parcel from home with all the good things we longed to have: lipstick, deodorants, cologne, bath powder, toothpaste, and other cosmetics that were unavailable in the jungle. A package for one meant something for everyone.

Recalling that period when my wardrobe had reached a dangerously low point, something quite comical happened one day. During our stop in Australia, I had purchased a new bra at a lingerie shop in Perth. It had no snaps or hooks on it because every ounce of metal in the country had been used in the war effort. It was put together with little cloth loops that fitted over buttons, cleverly constructed but insufficiently functional. At the most inappropriate times, the buttons would slip out of the loops and my anatomy would slip out of the bra. I could feel the unhinged garment falling around my waist, carrying with it my sense of propriety. In hopelessness, I threw the damn thing in the waste basket, this wartime garment that was too complex to get into and altogether too simple to get out of. Some time later, Mitzi and I were headed for the mess hall. Ahead of us were several Indians who worked in the area, men of a lower caste we thought, because they wore only the traditional *dhoti* over their loins. One of them wore a turban.

"Mitzi," I exclaimed, "am I seeing things, or is that my bra wrapped around that man's head?"

We walked fast to get closer to them, and there was no doubt. My old Australian bra had became a headdress for one of the barefoot natives who worked in the compound. He had artistically arranged for the buttons to appear directly over his forehead.

Chapter 15

Malaise at the 20th
General Hospital in Ledo

W E WERE ALL WAITING to hear what would happen next. Our *basha* was falling down around our ears, and the rats were getting more abundant, if that was possible. At night, they were clearly silhouetted against the walls as they raced back and forth on the bamboo poles between the burlap and the woven bamboo. We pledged never to bring anything edible into the building, but it soon became apparent that they were eating the building itself. Great holes appeared in the burlap and even in the bamboo partitioning. I shivered with the thought of how easy it would be to nibble an opening into the flimsy mosquito netting.

There was now a minimum of effort to keep the hospital functioning on the level we had previously kept it going; every activity was directed toward its closing. We wanted to give the bed sheets from the American wards to the Indians, but the British rejected this. Most of the equipment that might have been put to good use was destroyed. We heard excuses like "raise the standard of living," "increase black market activities," and "stimulate inflation." To someone like me, who practically had a Ph.D. in frugality, this sounded ridiculous. If an old bra could become a useful garment, think of the *dhotis* that could be made from bed sheets!

Our chief nurse called us all together one day. In her hand were orders for each nurse. The expectation of what might be printed on that little sheet of paper was mighty exciting. Several of the nurses had sufficient points to be sent directly to the ZI (zone of the interior, a wonderful euphemism for HOME). The point system was established to determine who was most eligible for mustering out, going home, or new assignments—so many points for being married, for length of time in service, for length of time overseas, for time in combat zones and so on. A few of the nurses were sent directly to Calcutta to the 142nd General Hospital, and a few of us, Mitzi included, were sent nineteen miles down the road to the 20th General Hospital in Ledo. That was an awful letdown, but at least we were getting away from that wilderness of decaying *bashas* and rampaging rats.

The hospital where we were going was the first to arrive in the theater, along with the troops who were to build the Ledo Road. The unit, formed at the University of Pennsylvania, was made up of the elite in the medical profession and had a staff of highly skilled nurses as well. The commanding officer of the hospital was Colonel Isidor Ravdin, who, on the recommendation of General Stilwell, was to become the first medical reserve officer ever to be promoted to brigadier general. No sooner had they arrived in this remote jungle than they began operating for the benefit of the road builders, the service personnel, and the combat forces. Here, in the middle of the most primitive circumstances, was a medical service with the very latest knowledge and techniques to alleviate the pain and suffering of all Allied servicemen in the area, American, Chinese, British and Indian. The evacuation, field and station hospitals in the area were all satellites of this large general hospital.

General Stilwell routinely visited his wounded and sick troops at the 20th General. When he saw how the typhus patients suffered in the heat and humidity, he ordered fans to be brought in, even several air-conditioned units, to bring maximum comfort to the men. The people at SEAC, the Southeast Asia Command, headquarters, never did know what happened to the fans from their offices. Among the thousands of soldiers treated at the 20th, were Major General Frank Merrill of the famous Marauders who suffered two heart attacks in the field. The most illustrious patient was Vice-Admiral Lord Louis Mountbatten, commander of all of SEAC. He, with Stilwell, was touring the battlefield at Walawbum after the nasty encounter with the Japanese there in the wild, wet Burmese jungle, when he ran a bamboo splinter in his eye. He underwent surgery at the 20th General, an operation that saved his vision in that eye. Excellent medical service and nursing care were not limited to prestigious names; it was doled out equally to every wounded or sick GI in the theater.

Mitzi and I fervently hoped we would be assigned to work with the patients here. We knew that staying busy was more desirable than hanging in limbo, waiting for that huge, impersonal organization called the Army to make a decision that would filter through myriad layers of bureaucratic nonsense before anything would happen to change our lives.

We were not alone at the 20th. Personnel from all the medical units in the CBI were coming down from the hills and valleys of Assam and Burma. Everyone was being processed—another word for standing in line—for return to the States or for reassignment. In another queue, I saw a face that was wonderfully familiar. I burst from my position in the line and ran across the compound to embrace a nurse who had been my first roommate back at the little hospital in the coal mining region of Pennsylvania. We had begun our nursing education at the same time, graduated together, and joined the Nurse Corps soon after that. She had been assigned to a field hospital in Shingbwiyang, at the head of the Hukawng Valley in Burma. This was the place where General Stilwell had established his headquarters when he initiated the push to drive the Japanese out of the country. Located in the extreme northwest corner, it was the only place in Burma where the enemy had not infiltrated and dug in. The Ledo Road construction had been completed up to Shingbwiyang, making it possible to bring supplies in trucks and jeeps to the troops who were engaged in battle just ahead of the road builders. Considering that Americans were scattered over the face of the earth by their participation in the war, I thought it a rare happenstance that we two women who had once shared such a common experience should meet in this distant unlikely place. Her name was Helen Goller, a tall, slender brunette who exemplified the highest qualities in the profession. She had always seemed tireless to me, able to do with two hands what others took four hands to accomplish. As student nurses, we had worked together caring for the coal miners who came for medical and surgical treatment. Their injuries were almost always severe: burns from explosions, fractures from falling rock, crushed bodies from collapsing mine ceilings, and mutilations from machinery that gouged out the valuable black anthracite that, in those days, was more widely used than oil for fuel. Nursing patients who suffered these traumas was grueling labor, but Helen, with her long arms and willowy frame could move the patients with heavy casts as smoothly as any nurse I knew, bathe their hurting bodies and rub their aching backs. We hugged with the special fondness that old roomies have for each other, then exchanged stories, especially about what was happening at home, not here in India. We reminisced about our early student days at Moses Taylor Hospital, about times when we were so exhausted from the long hours and hard work we could scarcely drag ourselves out of bed in the morning, and how we all pitched in and hurried like little beavers when there weren't enough nurses to care for the influx of patients. We both agreed that nursing in thatched roof buildings, caring for Oriental soldiers, coping with the ugliness of life in the jungle, was something neither of us had been prepared to do. Our isolation had been so complete that we didn't know where our classmates were or what they were doing. More than half the women in our small class of sixteen had joined the service, either the Army or the Navy Nurse Corps.

Mitzi's and my hopes for being assigned nursing duties at the 20th General evaporated when we were put on temporary duty, our only job being to wait, to wait, to wait, and try to stay on this side of sanity. Idleness was sometimes painful, and for some people it was dangerous because the vacuum it created could so easily be filled with debauchery. There was now a surfeit of nurses gathered in this one place, and our services were not required. Patients were being sent to the ZI (home), and those who needed more care were relocated to Calcutta and Karachi. We expected any day to get new orders, but the days stretched into weeks and we were obliged to make the best of it.

We lived in a barracks where privacy was non-existent. Army life had been an insult to my modesty and to that of many other of the women. One girl, quite uninhibited for that generation, walked about the barracks stark naked except for a pair of CBI boots. She was really a very regular girl. Her penchant for nudity embarrassed some of us, but I will say she probably was more comfortable in that climate than we were. I was always uneasy with the possibility of having a male officer knock on the barracks door, then walk in, because the door was always open. Nakedness was a taboo in my growing up years, and it was further impressed upon me as a student nurse, that exposing a patient unnecessarily was forbidden, a careless disregard for human dignity.

Idle time camaraderie: two nurses pretending to bathe in a garbage can.

Finding ways to fill the endless hours was a challenge, but I discovered early that it was important to keep active or else fall victim to that draining tropical lethargy. We played tennis, badminton, and ping-pong. We rode horses in the tea plantations and danced in the Officers' Club at the hospital, and best of all, there was a small library for the hospital's personnel where we were welcome to enjoy their books. Music from America was part of our lives. The songs that belonged to this era—"Don't Sit Under the Apple Tree with Anyone Else But Me," "Mairzy Dotes," "I'll Be Seeing You in All the Old Familiar Places," and many others—were the melodies that reminded us of home. I wondered about "Darling, Je Vous Aime Beaucoup." Had some GI in France fallen in love with a French girl? Why did these songs trigger the inconsolable longings that filled this wasteland of unstructured time. Underneath our grousing and our carefree pleasures, there was the certainty that our days in the Orient were numbered, that our country's military victory was a reality, and that we had only to conduct our lives in an acceptable fashion until we received orders to move on. I wrote letters to Pennsylvania and to Liangshan, the former filled with plans of what I'd do when I got home, the latter filled with girlish expressions of affection. Mail call was the high point of every day, but there was a dearth of letters coming through. Movements of various units from one place to the other was causing much misdirection in the flow of mail. Nothing came down from China, not a letter, not a note, not a message. Then one day I saw Red's commanding officer in the mess.

"Major, what a surprise to see you here in Ledo. What's up?" I felt certain he would have news for me.

"Not much. The squadron's still in Liangshan, but I'm on my way home." This news didn't do much to make me feel good. Red had told me, before he left, that he'd heard the 317th was getting a new commanding officer, and this confirmed the rumor. I began to have the sinking feeling that everything in my existence was an illusion, that I had been deceived into believing that a wartime romance could endure the vicissitudes of military life. Had I been assigned to work, to practice my nursing skills where the sick and wounded lay recovering and longing for home, I would surely have not suffered that terrible emptiness that preoccupied my waking hours. The boredom seemed as thick as the heat; the despair as heavy as the humidity. I itched to do more with my energies than sweat on the tennis court.

Many of the medical officers from the 14th Evac. came to the 20th General when we did. They had nothing to do and were forced to wait for further orders as we were doing. Tex was among these men, and I was glad to have such a good companion for riding the splendid horses that the British maintained in the region. We were closer to the tea plantations here in Ledo, perfect terrain for enjoying a gentle trot or a brisk canter. Another of our physicians was a captain whose insepa-rable comrade was a small monkey who perched himself on the cap-tain's shoulder and remained there day in and day out. The monkey was served a drink whenever the captain drank and both of them were eternally in a state of inebriation. Drinking was a way of life for many military men and women; probably a route of escape from the miseries that belong to overseas assignments.

Mitzi came flying into the barracks one afternoon with the news that Tom was leaving for home, back to England, the shattered little island that was the symbol of bravery and resolve. The freedom that we valued so much, that had tottered on the edge of a frightening abyss, had been held there with the stiff upper lip of the British. Mitzi was wild about Tom. His leaving was an excruciating trauma for her, a hurt that she thought could be alleviated with gin. After her good-byes were said, she embraced a bottle of Beefeater with the same ten-derness that she must have felt for Tom. Our barracks smelled like a grog house, and Mitzi was out of commission for several days. Poor lass! We all tried to dissuade her from drinking so much, for this was not really her pattern of conduct. She was never given to excesses before, but Tom's departure was a loss she couldn't handle. As I observed her behavior, I was reminded of something, an admonition squirreled away in my idealistic young soul, counsel given to me a long time ago before I had left for this assignment in the CBI.

The Presbyterian minister in whose home I had spent my ado-lescent years, where I helped to care for his children and performed simple household chores in return for a place to live while I went to high school, had said something to me that had had a profound impact. He had joined the armed forces as a chaplain and was assigned to a troop ship that sailed through the Pacific, transporting men to every port on the Pacific rim and to all the islands in the campaign. His home base was San Francisco, and while I was at Camp Beale he con-tacted me and we met at the Presidio. Together, we had dinner on Fisherman's Wharf. In the strangeness of my new environment and new life style, it was a thrill to see this man who had been a father figure in my formative years. I revered his person and respected his wisdom. While we dined, he told me what it was like to be a military chaplain. He had a deep concern for the young men who were thrust into war, torn from their roots, far from their families, fearful of never returning home, but he wasn't certain that what he said to them was very comforting. He told me that listening was the most effective way to help troubled soldiers.

"One of the great tragedies that I have encountered in this war," he said, "is young people becoming the kind of persons that they never planned to be. Away from the censuring eyes of their families and their communities, many of them have not been able to make good choices. Some of them drink too much, seek sexual pleasure without commitment, even cheat and lie and do many things that they would never do were they in their own territory. Most of them are brave and honorable, of course, but it does hurt me to see so many fine young men mess up their lives because of this pervasive feeling of 'anything goes.'"

As I had always done, I listened intently to what he said. He reached over the table, placed his hand on mine and spoke with great solemnity, "Vonny, don't let this happen to you."

As I watched Mitzi and sympathized with the inevitable termination of her romance with Tom, I thought about what Jim Bryden, the minister, had said to me. I was seeing, on a small scale, what he saw in endless measure. Of all the excesses that I saw, drinking was the most pervasive; all leisure time activity revolved around the consumption of alcohol. Patters of reckless behavior were easy to fall into, and for young women in the service it was a career just to hang on to one's chastity.

We learned from the nurses at the 20th that our own Ingrid who had been their patient had returned home. She had been diagnosed as having dengue fever. This, like malaria, was transmitted by the bite of a mosquito. She was completely well by the time she left.

Orders began to filter down from headquarters. We were weeded out for return to the States or for another assignment in the theater. Mitzi and I and a few other nurses were ordered to report for duty at the 142nd General Hospital in Calcutta, a transfer that we had anticipated since neither of us had very many "points," at least not enough to have the good fortune of being sent to the ZI. After weeks of doing nothing, we were eager to get on with being nurses again.

At the airstrip in Ledo, a place that held blissful memories for me, we boarded a C-47, that sturdy old workhorse that had contributed so much to the effort in the CBI as well as the other theaters of war. The bucket seats and the shabby, well used interior, reminded me of

Kismet, and as we rose over the airfield and headed for Calcutta, I knew that a chapter of my life was ending.

We said farewell forever to the wild up-country of Assam, where the hills, fissured with enormous gorges, thundering waterfalls, forests filled with leopards, tigers, monkeys and other exotic wildlife, would lie in the heart of my memory like an accursed jewel. For me, Assam signified the depth of my personal fear and despair on one hand, and the height of my joy and expectation on the other. Sloshing through the mud and monsoon downpours to minister to Chinese soldiers, living with physical discomforts so enfeebling to one's vigor, exposed to dark terrors stalking the jungle, constantly in fear of the debilitating diseases that waited at every bend for the opportunity to strike—these were the things I would remember. Transcending all these and more was the lingering fever that burned in my heart, the ardor that had overtaken me, the love of the red-haired airman whom I had known so briefly. Together we had soared over the cruelest mountains on the earth's crust, we had tasted the bitter flavor of an Oriental society wandering in its ragged dignity, we had wallowed in the haughty security of our Americanism, we had shared a moment in history that bound us together in a most unusual way. And yet, I had no way of knowing whether he, far away in China, harbored the same fervent feelings as I did.

There was considerable concern as to what America's role would be in China, especially since the governments of Chungking and Yenan were already engaged in sporadic conflicts. The risk of becoming involved in that nation's civil strife was great. Chiang Kai-shek expected us to equip and support his armies now that wartime lend-lease matèriel was no longer being provided. The Communists, under Mao Tse-tung, had rejected the corrupt government of Chiang Kai-shek. They felt that Chiang could not hold on to power for very long, no matter how much assistance he got from the United States. In the short term, the need for air transport in China was great. Chinese troops had to be transported to the coastal cities to take over the governments that had just been wrested from the Japanese. The enemy had controlled some of these city governments for as long as fifteen years; re-establishing the Chinese in the governing offices was not an easy task. It was a race between the Nationalists and the Communists to see who could get there first. Even our carrying those Chinese military men who had fought side by side with the Americans, appeared externally to be a gesture of support of the Nationalists. Added to that transportation need, all the Japanese who had occupied the land had to be repatriated. We did not want to become embroiled in a "fratricidal war" but America was in a cold sweat at the thought of the Communists taking over this vast country. We had deployed thousands of Marines to North China to occupy the cities until the Nationalists got there to accept the Japanese surrender. I didn't know what the 317th Troop Carrier Squadron was assigned to do. I only knew that Red was there, and if we ever met again he would tell me what he had been up to.

Chapter 16

A Regular Army Nurse
at the 142nd General Hospital

THIS WAS THE third time I had been in Calcutta, but this time I
was not a visitor. I was a functioning staff member of a large military medical complex that had been in existence since our involvement in war on the Asian mainland. Calcutta was a port of entry for
supplies for the whole theater, and particularly for Assam which was
the jumping off place for everything that went to Chiang Kai-shek for
the defense of China. With all of coastal China under the thumb of
the enemy, Calcutta was the back door that could receive matériel and
ship it to the airfields in Assam from whence the ATC carried it over
the mountains to Kunming, Chungking, or wherever there was a base
to receive it. Along with war matériel came American servicemen and
women. They were thrust into an environment that demanded constant vigilance against disease for this was a place where hygienic practices as we knew them, were nonexistent.

The medical department of the United States Army had been
faced with a grave problem when American troops were committed to
this theater of war. Troops assigned to the CBI had to depend entirely
on their own sanitary discipline and their practices of preventive medicine, or they could not survive in the culture that existed here. No food
and no water could be obtained safely from any source in the local
community. James H. Stone wrote a report on the medical service in
the theater for the Office of the Surgeon General in which he made
this comment:

> Milk, for example, that reached an eating establishment or a
> home in India, invariably had been thoroughly contaminated

with canal, ditch, river or rain water, which in turn had been polluted by human excrement. Native abattoirs were usually open courtyards where clouds of dust and dried manure filled the air, animals were tethered to await slaughter, blood and wastes were trampled underfoot, and dogs and vultures snatched at entrails under the very hands of the butchers. Vegetables came to the market well sprinkled with human excrement; by the time they reached the consumer they were often desiccated or rotten.

Each of us had a responsibility to keep ourselves well and disease free as far as it was in our power to do so. We purposely avoided exposure to the filth of Calcutta, drank only water that we knew had been boiled, and were careful where and what we ate. I envied the nurses who had been assigned to the European theater where they might comfortably eat in a local restaurant where the preparation of food was more often in the western tradition.

The 142nd General Hospital had been established early in the war but when I was assigned to nursing duty there, it was still a seventeen hundred bed facility. Originally, the British and some wealthy Indians had turned over their splendid palaces for use as medical institutions. As the need arose, the Americans added barracks to house the patients and the staff. What had once been a spacious civilian park gradually filled up with military buildings, edifices that were unbecoming to the beautiful street, Southern Boulevard, where they had been erected. Some of the nurses lived in the "Pink Palace" where marble floors and bathtubs must have made them feel like maharanees, but I was not fortunate enough to have a room there.

I lived in a barracks with sixteen other nurses. There were other barracks, too, and they were all lined up perpendicular to a long covered ramp that functioned as a verandah. We could sit on this open porch in the peaceful Indian evenings and listen to the hum of the cicadas, the softly padding bare feet of Indian servants, and quiet conversation. It was now late in the year, the best time to be in Calcutta, for the days were sunny and warm, the nights cool and gentle. When Red and I had that splendid interlude, that escape from the jungle, the city was suffocating in summer heat and humidity, accentuating every abominable feature of life in Calcutta.

As was the custom, I hired a personal servant, an ayah who belonged to the Sudras (the caste of laborers and serving people). Lila (I called her Lily) was a fragile adolescent Hindu girl who cleaned my shoes, carried my uniforms to the *dhobi wallah*, washed and pressed my personal clothing, made my bed—in other words, she waited on me hand and foot in much the same way that Corbi had done when I lived in a *basha* in Assam. This was a luxury that I had never experienced in my own country; indeed, if a servant were involved in anything that went on in life back home, it was I who was the servant. But here I was *mem-sahib*, a status that brought pleasure tainted with guilt, while I was living in this nation at a time when dark skin was always subservient to white skin. It was easy to become addicted to having simple tasks performed by someone else, to leave mundane concerns and menial work to the attention of a servant. Sometimes when I looked at Lily's delicate face, I thought I detected a smoldering resentment in her sullen black eyes. The spontaneous laughter and gaiety that I had seen in the Chinese was nowhere present among the Indians that I dealt with here in Calcutta.

After weeks of waiting, hours of packing and unpacking, interminable repositioning, it was a relief and a gratification to go on duty. It had been a long time since I had headed up a nursing unit made up of our own GIs, for most all hospitalized men at the 14th Evac. were Chinese. The bush clothes, high top shoes, long pants and long sleeves were a thing of the past. We wore the brown and white seersucker wrap-around dresses that made us look dowdy but were nevertheless very comfortable. The relaxed attitude that had overtaken us up in the hills was replaced with more rigid military discipline. We reported on duty in meticulously proper dress, cap in place, and all ensignia accurately displayed according to regulations. Our principal chief nurse was regular Army, not at all like the motherly woman who, back at the 14th Evac., treated us like her Girl Scout troop. The simple "Good morning, Lieutenant" greeting was replaced with silence and a snappy salute. We worked from seven o'clock in the morning until one in the afternoon, or from one until seven in the evening. Night duty was still a twelve hour shift.

I was sometimes assigned to an isolation ward where we had tuberculosis patients and at other times to a unit of young men with poliomyelitis. There had been an outbreak of polio among the troops somewhere in the theater, and the 142nd was better equipped than most other theater hospitals to handle those patients who had residual paralysis. We had several iron-lungs, clumsy things compared to today's respirators.

Asepsis and isolation technique was one nursing function in which I was highly proficient. After the wonderfully effective anti-bacterial drugs came into common use, there was considerable relaxation in the rigidity of aseptic practices, but with the advent of AIDS there is a return to the emphasis on flawless techniques. As a student, I had often been first scrub nurse for the surgeons at Moses Taylor Hospital and had been schooled in the pediatric unit at the New York Hospital in isolation techniques where every child was protected from cross infection by some measure, depending upon what was indicated. All my efforts to do things correctly with the Chinese had failed miserably, for they did not understand the concepts of the transmission of disease, and the equipment for carrying out the procedures was not available in that primitive setting. Here, at last, I could practice my chosen profession with a degree of skill that would bring the personal satisfaction that is the reward of hard work well done. Added to the efforts to prevent the spread of infection, our goal was to make these patients as comfortable as possible, help them to get an "up-beat" feeling about life and send them home as quickly as possible. Listening was probably the most effective of our functions, for these men needed to articulate the rage that seethed inside them as well as to express the hope they harbored for recovery. We tried to reinforce their positive feelings and play down their despair. If I remember one thing about the American GI who was hospitalized, it was his irrepressible resiliency. He seemed able to recover when all the medical facts pointed otherwise.

Another group of patients that I attended were the prisoners of war that were being brought in from the camps in Burma, Malaysia, and from down in the valley of the Kwai where the Japanese had held them for years. They had been bullied and beaten, starved and forced to labor in silent humiliation. Most of them felt fortunate to be alive, for they had witnessed the demise of their fellow prisoners at the hands of men who felt that the importance of an individual man's life was "of no more account than a feather." These men had survived a long night of fear and hope, and hope had won in the battlefield of their minds, but the cost of those years would leave a scar that could not be excised from their spirits. Their listlessness was a contradiction to the wild, haunted look in their eyes. While they had tried to keep alive a consciousness of the world outside their prison environment, now that they had entered that world they were uncomfortable and self-conscious. I was keenly aware of these prisoners' reluctance to talk, so kept a respectful silence as I ministered to their bodies. When they did speak, they never expressed invidiousness toward their captors; they talked of what it would be like to be home once more, England and Scotland being home to some of them. It was not in the personality of most Americans to hate, but after seeing these pathetic prisoners of war, I came as close to feeling intense loathing for the Japanese as I had ever felt toward anyone. To myself, I was saying the worst things I could think of about them: buck-tooth bastards, yella-bellied scoundrels, dirty-rotten Nips!

Malaria was rampant in the prisoners, but there were other things more obvious. They were appallingly emaciated. Many had lost some or all of their teeth and starvation had affected their vision. I remember one man who had an infection at the base of every nail so that the ends of his fingers were swollen and distorted. I expected that they would eat ravenously, but such was not the case. They looked at the food, ate part of it and often tried to save the remainder, as though they would not be served a meal again that day. The nursing care that I gave to these prisoners of war gave me the greatest satisfaction I had ever had, for I could feel them respond to the gentle touch that spoke of caring in a way far more eloquent than any words. As I cleansed their sores and applied dressings, I watched their faces, hoping for a smile or for conversation, but usually there was only grim passiveness.

Inside the hospital compound, the practice of medicine and the nursing of patients went on in a spotlessly clean environment. Just at the fringes of the park where the hospital stood was the boundary of a totally different world. One day, in the course of my daily nursing chores, I stopped to look through the fence that had been erected around the periphery of the hospital barracks. On the other side of this open wire wall, I watched as a *dhoti* clad Indian washed his ox. He had a bucket of water and a cloth which he repeatedly dipped into the water, swabbed the flanks of the beast, washing away all the dust and filth accumulated on the hide of the patient animal. When he had finished, he began washing himself. With the same water, the same dirty rag, and the same deliberate action, he washed his face, his arms, his torso, reached under his *dhoti* to wash his genitals, wiped his thighs and legs and poured a little of the remaining water on his feet. Then— I couldn't believe my eyes—he lifted the bucket to his lips and drank.

Working was the greatest panacea for the torture of waiting to return home. All the hospitals in the CBI that had not been closed were shrinking. What we expected to happen was this sequence: orders for return to the States, a well-deserved leave, and then reassignment to one of the bulging veterans' hospitals. We were just marking time, but it was very satisfying to go to work every day and practice those nursing skills that we felt had grown rusty.

In the meantime, there were many hours with not much to do in a city that had few familiar elements in its makeup. In the hospital compound, there was a movie theater for the troops, an Officers' Club and tennis courts, but not much else. Sometimes we would take reading material to the little grassy plot in the back of our barracks and lie on a blanket while we read. Always, high above, the vultures would begin a circling pattern of flight, gradually descending to see whether the flesh that was lying in the sun was food for their insatiable appetites. We would lie perfectly still until the scavengers were practically upon us, then we would move, change position, and dash their hopes for a meal. They would ascend and repeat the same downward spiral, over and over.

"Mitzi, those buzzards are waiting for us to die," I remarked one day.

"The way I feel, they won't have to wait long," she groaned. We were both homesick, both had romances that seemed dead—Tom gone back to his Yorkshire farm and Red up in Liangshan, silent and not communicating.

"It's high time we found some interesting guys," Mitzi said. "There are some neat clubs in this city. We've gotta get to them while we're here. I don't expect ever to come to Calcutta again as long as I live, so now's the time."

"Well, I don't feel much like hanging around waiting for Hot Shot Charlie," I agreed. "He's probably back in the States cavorting with some wench that he knew before the war." I had given up hopes of hearing from him as most everyone was coming out of China so they could be home for the approaching holidays. I had many invitations to go out with the medical officers and other men who were trapped in this far off place and sought female companionship, but none of them interested me in quite the inexplicable way that Red did.

"Have you had mail from home?" Mitzi asked.

"I had a letter from my sister saying that Bill had been shipped back from China. He's home. Imagine! And my Mom wrote that the snow is a foot deep in Pennsylvania." The word "snow" brought on a sudden attack of acute longing for all the familiar scenes of my childhood, or perhaps for childhood itself. In my dreaming, the farm had taken on storybook qualities of pastoral beauty, when in fact, it remained a rustic, marginal enterprise, providing such a meager living that my family were really rural paupers. Surely other men and women who were absent from home for a long time created images in their minds that far surpassed the realities that they had left behind. These distortions were comforting to me, gave me confidence and security that I needed to see me through this difficult time. I was supposed to be, at age twenty-one, grown up, mature, responsible, competent to make adult decisions, self-reliant and independent. Honest introspection found other qualities: insecurity, indecision and irresolution. Fortunately, I was very good at putting on a deceptive facade.

Chapter 17

Life in Calcutta

M ITZI HAD SEEMINGLY recovered from her romance with Tom and was accepting dates from whomever would take her to the most desired places: the British American Club, the Gymkhana Club, Firpo's—to name a few. Among the army people left in the theater, there was an atmosphere of recklessness, a keen desire to snatch pleasure wherever it could be found. We recognized that there was little time left before the realities of life in America would be upon us, that we'd be faced with making decisions about our careers, that this atmosphere of escapism would soon evaporate. Life appeared to be free of pressures.

The social life of the English ebbed and flowed in tempo with the condition of the empire. Now that the war was over it appeared that the attempt to recover "the good old days" was underway, but deep down, everyone knew that nothing would ever be the same again in this teeming city, nor in any other part of India. The masses had toned down their cries for independence while Japan threatened the continent, but now that the Japanese were vanquished, the populace was straining against the ties that bound them to that small green island on the other side of the glove. For some reason, Mitzi was inclined to seek companionship with the British rather than our own officers, so she began to date a man from the Royal Navy who was temporarily based in Calcutta. I was introduced to an officer from the ATC, a young man whom I found to be good company as well as a splendid dancer. In a cosmopolitan city such as this, it was a pleasure to know someone to go to the clubs with. We were always engaged in things that were American as we consciously separated ourselves from things that were foreign. I had no letters from Liangshan. Thinking about Red was painful, so I filled my hours with work, with evenings of dancing and "clubbing," with day excursions to the bazaars, with anything that diverted my attention from the appearance that I was no longer important to the "fly boy" who had waggled his wings into my life, then flew off into China, never to be heard from again.

One of the favorite night spots that the officers enjoyed was the British American Club. On the route we drove to get there was a long brick wall covered with cow-patties, the dung of the sacred cows, formed into little round pancake-shaped dabs and stuck onto the wall to dry. As mentioned before, these were used for fuel by the lower caste Indians, many of whom cooked their scavenged morsels right on the street. They wrapped the food in a leaf, then set it in the burning cow dung until it was cooked, then ate it, always with their right hand. Someone told me that these "untouchables" used the left hand to clean themselves after defecating, so the right hand was considered proper to use for eating. Talk about not having one hand know what the other is doing! Along the sides of the streets there was always the blue smoky stench of burning cow-patties, squatting Indians eating their meager meals, and sacred cows searching for a rare blade of grass. Our dates who took us to the club joked about giving any nurse who had made three trips there, the cow-patty cluster, a satirical imitation of the Oak Leaf Cluster which was a military decoration for valor or distinguished service.

Evenings spent in the clubs were fun because we usually met people who had crossed our paths at other times and in other places. Sometimes they had news of friends who had been up in the jungles with us, and they often knew who had returned to the States or had been reassigned. Someone you had not met before might invite you to have a *chota-peg* (a drink) and before long you found that you had mutual friends in India. The American community in Calcutta was restive, for we harbored the perception that our country was less interested in the China or the India-Burma theaters—the CBI had been split into two separate theaters by this time—than in the European theater and that the efforts to bring us home were not as urgent as for the heroes of Anzio, Monte Casino, Paris, and Berlin. To this day, I believe there has been less documentation of the war in Asia than the war in Europe. Whenever we were "sweating out" orders, it seemed necessary to have someone to blame for the delays, so we griped and groused but we didn't let our youthful spirits shrivel. We explored the city.

I became accustomed to things that once seemed appalling: to the odors, to dust, to filth, to the endless begging for *baksheesh*, to the rattle of rickshaws and the strident voices of merchants, to the wildly driven cabs and their constant honking, to the bony-ribbed cows, to the red spit left everywhere by the Indians who chewed betel nut, to the fragile men and women forever washing themselves at the standpipes where water trickled forth, to rotting heaps of garbage just around the corner from an ostentatious palace of a wealthy citizen, to the sad eyes that carry the depth of human despair in their blackness. I learned to avert my senses from the realities that enveloped me, holding at arm's length the pitiful human situation that seemed unrelated to me and my status as an American.

We were advised against two particular things when we left the hospital to go into the city. One was riding in a *tikka-gharri* and the other was visiting the bazaars, two adventures that were high on our list simply because they must have been exceedingly interesting if we were supposed not to do them. Mitzi and I felt it would be safer to go with our dates as two girls without escorts might seem easy prey for beggars or thieves.

John, the ATC fellow whom I was now dating, and I climbed into the *gharri* a small box-like cart drawn by a small horse or pony. Because the cart was completely closed in with only a small horizontal slit to see through, it was considered a place where evil could occur and no one would be able to see. You could be robbed or ravaged inside this little enclosed vehicle, and who could hear your summons for help? The minute I entered the vehicle I wished that I had not. It reeked of the odor of rancid fat and stale perspiration and probably urine as well. Because no air was admitted into the cramped little cubicle, both John and I felt we would die of respiratory failure before the *gharri* got to the bazaar, for that is where we told the driver to take us. The open rickshaws, drawn by the barefoot men of the street, were far more comfortable than the *tikka-gharri* so I never again hired a ride in one of those dreadful contraptions. When we alighted at the bazaar, I felt that I had stepped into another century. Row upon row of tiny shops lined the passageways and in the middle space the merchants squatted over their little circular piles of merchandise. They greeted us with that graceful gesture, the salaam, folded hands raised as in prayer. I learned that the height of the raised hands was an indication of the importance of the person being salaamed, hands raised to the forehead for a very prestigious person, to only the lips for a lesser man. Our salaams were from the lips.

The noise of the bazaar was truly an orchestration of sounds peculiar to this immense and complex country: the songs that form in the back of the throat then come out via the nasal passages; the sound of bells, all high pitched and tiny; the wrangling of sellers and buyers; the call of birds; the scuffing of goats' feet in the dust. Hundreds of sounds floated over the incessant motion of the Indian people, endless in their variety. They cooked over their little fires and the air was filled with the smell of mustard oil, curry and many spices that I did not know. I bought some silver, bracelets and a ring. I later found out that the ring I had purchased was made precisely for prostitutes. It was a cluster of little silver blobs attached to the circular part that wrapped around the finger. These blobs produced a definite kind of noise when you shook your finger. The woman who wore the ring would walk by a prospective customer and shake the ring to get attention; if he was interested in what she had for sale, he would follow where she led him. The number of shops and the acres of goods spread out to be sold was overwhelming, and as we wandered around I felt there was a great possibility of getting lost in this labyrinth of dusty, well-trodden paths.

We visited the New Market. This was a bazaar too, but it was more like a giant supermarket and lacked the atmosphere that the authentic one had. There was an effort in the New Market to emulate the world of western merchandising, but they failed miserably. The ceiling was hung with great bunches of bananas, and baskets of fruit were stacked in tiers. Sometimes a man could be seen sleeping soundly among the piles of produce. Butchers displayed meat in a way that was certain to turn a stomach upside-down. Carcasses of the beast hung from the rafter, the head rolling to the side showing a protruding tongue, the glazed eyes fixed in an expression of alarm, even the tail still attached to the spine. This, I thought, is unrelated to eating; it is a reminder of killing. When chops or steak or other cuts of meat are displayed in a bed of ice, with a sprig of parsley, that is when a mind turns to food and the pleasure of a good meal, but when hung haphazardly in an open area, it is the essence of a slaughter. The flies swarmed over everything. The staring eyes of the butchered sheep were rimmed with flies, the bloody tissues of muscle and bone were blackened with flies, the fruit and vegetables had rotting patches where the flies gathered in circles of moving wings. We did not linger in this place, even though the New Market was considered one of the best marketing centers in the city of Calcutta. Food was not all that was sold there, for it was an outlet for India's superb cottons, its interesting brass fixtures and cookware, and its unsurpassed tea.

Although we knew better than to eat food that was not prepared in our own mess, meals served at the great cosmopolitan hotels or in the better clubs were generally safe. Firpo's, on Chowringhee, could put out a divine dinner and the atmosphere of the place was well worth the trip. Two things I allowed myself to have: the small red bananas that grew locally, and the enormous cashew nuts that were also native grown. In the clubs, an *hors d'oeuvre* was served that I had never eaten before nor have I ever seen since. Surely there is a proper name for this delicious tidbit, but I don't know what it is. I can only describe what I recall—little triangular pillows of flaky, cheese flavored pastry-like layers which were so rich that they took one's appetite away. They were served with the refreshing lime drinks readily available in this country, drinks that tasted cold, even though there was never enough ice.

There were some times when we were advised to stay off the streets of Calcutta, for the populace was in great upheaval. Mohandas Gandhi had championed the cause of independence for India and at last these people were asserting their desire to rid the nation of England's colonial rule. He espoused noncooperation with the existing government and nonviolence in the resistance. Underlying the movement for independence was the irreconcilability of the Muslin-Hindu points of view. It reminded me, in a small way, of the rift between the Nationalists and the Communists in the Chinese situation, but this clash was more profound because it involved the spiritual lives of these two religious sects. In China, the split had been merely political. Unfortunately, Mr. Gandhi's appeal for nonviolence was not heeded and periodic outbursts of rage brought periodic shedding of blood. I saw the running, torch-carrying mobs swell and overrun the streets and was fearful that I would be mistaken for a Britisher. "Oh, my," I thought, "must there always be revolution or war?" I had seen the unrest in China, and the unrest in India, and I thought how peaceful are the streets and the countryside in my own America.

As was happening in all the hospitals, the boys were going home.

For those who had to remain until proper transportation was available, the nurses did everything they could think of to accelerate their recovery and keep them happy. For a short time, I was assigned to one patient, a young officer who was in the iron-lung. He would have to be taken home by air, inside his breathing apparatus, as this would get him Stateside quickly. It took time for appropriate arrangements to be made, time that turned him into the meanest wretch I have ever nursed. It took the patience of Job to deal with his tantrums. I had to look beyond his behavior to the seriousness of his situation, and then give him the genuine compassion that he really deserved. He would never be the same man that came to this part of the world to serve his country, for he, like those who had vanished on the Hump, had given his life, or the better part of it.

On a soft and quiet evening, I came home from the mess and sat on that long ramp in front of my barracks. Some other nurses came and rested for a while, and the conversation always found a circuitous route to the heart of every matter—when do you think we'll be going home? We knew that as long as there was one patient left who needed nursing care here, we'd also be there, so our hopes were tied, in a way, to the patient census.

"Five of my patients were discharged today," one of the girls said. Others would report when their GIs or officers were taken out to board ship or driven to Dum Dum Airport.

"I am specializing one polio patient," I said, "and they just can't seem to find a way to get him home."

"It'll be soon," someone offered. "Be patient. Could be you'll fly home with him."

That thought had not occurred to me but it sounded like a wonderful possibility.

Chapter 18

Red Stops By

D ARKNESS FELL EARLY, but the porch was such a lovely spot that
I hated to give it up for the chatter of a dozen nurses in the barracks. Mitzi had gone out on a date. Overcome with the lassitude
that is a distinguishing feature of life in India, I continued to drink
in the hypnotizing quality of the tranquil night. Stars punctured the
deep, dark sky. The trees stood motionless, forming a canopy of cool
green over the ramp; my mind was as still as the night—no thought,
no dreams, just a sense of being alive at the most basic level. Then
far, far down the end of the long ramp I saw a figure move and the
sound of someone whistling softly, "Darling, Je Vous Aime Beaucoup." My heart skipped a beat—it couldn't be. I held my breath as
the figure continued to walk toward me, and then I knew. His cap
was pushed to the back of his head, and no one whistled that song
the way he did. I ran headlong into his arms with the most undignified
shriek of joy.

"Red! What are you doing here?"

"I'm on my way home, baby! We came down to Kunming yesterday and I gave Kismet to the Thai Air Force. No mama, no papa, no
airplane. *Baksheesh*, baby, gimme *baksheesh*," he pleaded, mimicking the
beggars, and he picked me off my feet, whirled me around as we both
laughed breathlessly at seeing each other again.

After the first sloppy gushes, wordlessness settled in. I felt the
emotional numbness of those weeks of feeling abandoned slip away,
replaced with pure panic. What now?

"Come, sit here," I invited, as this was as quiet a place as could be
found. "You're just passing through, then?" I asked.

"That's right. We're waiting for a ship to dock here in Calcutta,
and I dared to leave my unit and find where you were. I thought you

might have left already, but I'm glad you're still here. You could beat me home if you fly."

"If you don't miss the boat, you'll be home for Christmas," I commented, "but it looks like I'll be here until the hospital closes."

He pulled his Zippo lighter from his pocket and fumbled with a cigarette. In the brief blaze of the lighter I saw his blonde lashes framing his blue eyes and the boyish face that I had come to feel was the handsomest in the world.

We sat in the still evening for a long time while Red filled me in on what he had been doing. He and the squadron of troop carriers went to Liangshan to gather up the Americans who had been stationed in remote places throughout the interior of China. There were OSS people who, at the invitation of Mao Tse-tung, had been observers of the Communists up in Yenan. There were some of our own fighter pilots whose services were no longer needed. All these men were flown to staging areas and prepared for return to the States. If this was the major reason for their going to China, it did not consume all their hours, for Red was involved in a lot of things that seemed unrelated to official military purpose. They soon left Liangshan and moved north to Hsian.

"Our C.O. had a stripped down B-25 that he loved to fly around. In the morning, after we got the other planes off the ground and sent on their special assignments, he and I would take off to get a good look at the country. We flew over the Great Wall and beyond to the flat lands of inner Mongolia. You can't imagine the expanse of land up there—wild horses, nomadic people, mile upon mile of wide open space."

"Sounds to me as though you were just playing around, Red." I probably sounded disapproving, but it did seem that the army had a way of wasting our time and their money. In my own experience, I had had short periods of working myself to death, and then periods of resting myself to death. If anyone was working hard now, it was labor that would accelerate the evacuation of the theater. Everything had taken on a more relaxed tenor.

"One mission I flew didn't seem quite on the up and up," he told me. "A colonel and a major climbed aboard and with them they had two suitcases full of money."

"Where'd you take them?" I asked.

"We flew them out to the coast, to Shanghai. The exchange rate was such that they could quadruple their bucks in no time. They bought *yuan* in Hsian that was worth a lot more in Shanghai, then traded it all for American dollars. These guys explained the process to us, but the last thing they said was, 'You better not try it or you'll get in trouble.' I can't believe that what they were doing was condoned by our government."

"Getting rich in wartime has always been a game with some people," I commented. "I suppose everything up in China is pretty unstable—a great place for opportunists. Tell me what Shanghai was like." It was such a thrill to have Red spend a few hours with me, and the conversation we were having was so interesting that I dreaded the moment when word would come to order him aboard the ship bound for America. He seemed to be very eager to love me, but he was inarticulate and shy about such matters so it wasn't easy for me to know whether or not I fitted into his future plans.

This was the time when our country was making decisions about further action in China. Some of our leaders wanted to continue to support Chiang Kai-shek, but men who knew this complex country and its problems sensed that it was time to get out. General Stilwell was one of these men. He recognized that anything we could provide the Nationalist government would be ineffective because of the corruption in the Kuomintang.

"I flew two Chinese civilians from Hsian to Shanghai. I have no idea what they were doing but they told me their position in the Chinese government was the equivalent of our own FBI. They took me and my copilot to dinner at a swanky place on Nanking Road, about a half dozen blocks from the Bund."

"What's the Bund?"

"That's the big embankment down on the river in Shanghai. All the buildings there were built by Europeans in the days when they had control of China's ports and shipped goods out to the rest of the world. The restaurant was called the Sun Ya. You wouldn't believe the menu or the elegance of the place. The only people who dined there were the rich or the men in the high echelons of government."

"Like that place on the Ledo Road where we ate egg-foo-yung?" I asked jokingly, thinking of that first time we ate dinner in the smoky little shack.

Red (left) was at the surrender of the airfield in Peking. The Japanese were allowed to keep their weapons to secure the field against theft.

"Yeh. That seems like a lifetime ago, doesn't it?" I wondered if he was thinking about that first kiss. I was.

"After that we went to a night club in the city. Shanghai manages to keep its image as a very worldly place, in spite of the long Japanese occupation. There was a white Russian woman, a really beautiful female, working at her business among the men at the bar. The men who took us there told us to watch how she operated. She initiated conversation with some of the club's clients, then, when she apparently found someone who would pay the right price to sleep with her, she nodded to her husband. He could go home and wait while she earned the family's keep."

"That's a new twist to an old profession," I commented. "Is China filled with that kind of stuff?" I asked. Talking openly about something of this nature made me a bit uncomfortable, but it also affirmed my suspicion that war shatters the moral fiber of some men and women and alters the mores of a generation.

"China's filled with everything, Vonny, good, bad and unbelievable. While the Japanese controlled the eastern provinces, these people had rough times. Maybe that woman's activities were the only thing that made it possible for them to eat."

"We flew up to Peking. It was our command that accepted the surrender of the airfield from the Japanese. Our squadron was supposed to keep the airport secure until the Marines got there to occupy the whole city. We kept the Japanese armed so they could keep the Chinese from stealing everything that wasn't nailed down."

"That seems crazy—letting the Japs keep guns. I thought they were the vanquished," I commented.

"This Colt .45," Red went on, as he patted the pistol hanging from his weapon's belt, "brings twelve hundred dollars on the black market, so the Chinks are wild to get their hands on them. Our CO sent out the word that any officer who had his side arm stolen would be fined that amount."

"Bet you keep close tabs on that gun, don't you?"

"One of our pilots left his on the seat in the cockpit—just while he ran into the operations building for a minute. When he came out the gun was gone. He found out the CO wasn't kidding about the twelve hundred dollar fine."

"Peking was an interesting place. Our squadron's medical officer, Doc, was a real connoisseur of Chinese art and he wanted to see if he could find things to take home. We went to the motor pool where the Japanese had the latest model cars, checked out a big black Lincoln sedan and went downtown. We shopped in the city where the bargains were very tempting, but I don't know anything about what's of value and what isn't, so I didn't buy very much, but Doc had a field day spending money." Red was eager to tell me about his travels, probably because he knew they were finished and he was at last free to return to the normalcy of life in New Jersey.

"Doc and I went to a night club owned by a Japanese woman and a white Russian woman. We had a wonderful dinner of filet mignon and champagne. You won't believe this, but the dinner cost the equivalent of twenty-five cents, and the wine, the best that French monks make, was a dollar a quart. Inflation is becoming a serious problem in China. Makes the American dollar look like solid gold."

"Are any of the fellows from the 317th still up there?"

"Well our CO came down here with me, and the operations officers. Some of the men are still in China doing various things. One of our guys went down to Saigon and brought some prisoners here to your hospital. Then there's always a lot of brass having to be ferried here and there, but it won't be long now before the whole squadron is outbound, for home."

"Did you see the Forbidden City?"

"A bunch of us went there, but there was so much to look at, the place was so enormous we could have spent a week and not covered the same thing twice. We went out to the summer palace, too. Saw the empress Dowager's marble boat. China is really a country that is too big, too diverse to experience in weeks—a lifetime would be needed."

"One of the most thrilling moments of my whole tour of duty in China was when the Marines finally arrived in Peking."

"Why did you get such a kick out of that?" I asked.

"I really don't know why, but when I saw those guys I had the most violent attack of patriotism I'd ever had. The train rolled into the huge railroad station in the city, and a Marine band started to play 'The Marine Corps Hymn.'

"And then a whole battalion of leather-necks stepped out of those train cars, stood at attention looking just what Marines are supposed to look like, clean and sharp. Tough, too. Many of them had fought in the Pacific and were sent into China after those islands were secured. It was a sight. I could feel myself swelling with pride to be an American."

For someone who was quiet and not given to emotionalism, Red had talked more candidly about his feelings than ever before. I feasted my eyes on him while he related all these things to me. I was besotted with affection, but still there was no reason to think that this infatuation would survive the rigors of time and distance. He had stopped to see me on his way home. Even that gesture was a portent that we might meet sometime on the far shores of the U.S., but I had no reason to harbor fantasies of permanence.

"What about tomorrow? Can I see you?" Red asked the question that I was about to ask him.

"I have morning duty, but after one in the afternoon I'm free." I was wondering where we could go and what we might do that would be a fitting finale to a wonderfully rich relationship. "Let's have dinner at the British American Club, or Firpo's. You can probably get a jeep from the motor pool."

"Okay. I'll let you know if the transport ship leaves before tomorrow."

That was the longest night I ever spent, and the next morning my six hours of nursing duties seemed like a double shift. I couldn't wait to see Red, just to be near him, for that was the place where I felt more like the real me than anywhere else in the world. He was waiting for me on the long ramp outside my barracks. I changed from duty uniform to dress uniform and we headed out, hoping to find a jeep, but there was none available.

"We'll just take a rickshaw, Red," I suggested.

"Let's get one of those wild taxis, those big four door jobs that make so much noise." A ride in one of those old Phaeton sedans, touring cars they were called, was some experience. They were driven by a Sikh and another Sikh sat on the passenger side just to operate the horn. The horn looked like a bulb syringe, a rubber ball attached to a hollow brass speaker. When the bulb was squeezed, a raucous sound was forced out of the horn, and it was generously used during the whole ride. Of course, blowing the horn made little difference in getting the street cleared of pedestrians and cows, they sauntered in and out of the automobile's path as nonchalantly as ever. The driver stopped several times during the ride, stopped and went into a little shop on an obscure street—to get his fix, Red suggested. Everyone suspected that these drivers were addicted to some substance that didn't do much to enhance their ability to drive.

"You would think we were the king and queen, Red. Did you ever hear so much noise in your life?"

"Look over there," Red pointed out, "the mobs are gathering and they're getting agitated. I'll bet there will be some heavy rioting before this night is over," he warned.

We sat in the British American Club and drank gimlets and talked for hours. We talked about the things we planned to do when we got back to Uncle Sam. We talked about our families, our childhoods, which now seemed so far in the past. We were in our early twenties, one of the most endearing and loveliest times of life, but we felt as though middle-age had crept up on us in the long months of separation from our familiar environments. It was a relief to know that the war was over, but going home would be like going back to square one, and beginning life all over again.

"I was afraid you would have to stay in China, Red. It looks as though there will be all-out war there soon and Chiang is counting on us to save China from Communism. Did you get any feel for the situation when you were there?"

"Can't say that I did, but I did have one very strange assignment. I can't figure out what it was all about, but I had to fly two American civilians to a remote spot up in Yenan in the dark of night. Our orders were to have no communication with the two passengers. We were given a course to fly and the elapsed time and told that we would recognize the place to land as it would be lighted. My crew and I didn't know what to expect as we lifted off into unknown territory. I didn't know whether we were flying over mountains or rice paddies, I just followed the flight plan that they gave me. First thing you know we began to ice up. As the ice gathered on the wings, we began to lose altitude—scary feeling. We had flown the amount of time that the flight plan called for when, sure enough, there were some lights on the ground. I brought the plane down and circled around to see what was there. Except for a half dozen smudge pots to light an unpaved runway, there was nothing there. We landed. It was cold as the devil up there. Then I saw a little tar-paper shack. Two men with kerosene lanterns were standing outside the building and began to approach the plane. They were dressed in those blue padded uniforms that we saw up in Hsian. Remember? Our two passengers alighted and met these other two guys, and they all went inside the miserable little shack. There wasn't another thing in sight, just flat desolate terrain in every direction. We waited for about an hour while those four men did what they had to do—probably something to do with the Communists since it all happened in their territory.

"Were your passengers military people or civilians?" I asked.

"They were dressed in civvies, but who knows what they were. Pretty soon they all came out of the building, two of the men holding up their lanterns to light the way to the plane. Our two passengers climbed aboard and we flew back to Hsian."

"What do you think it was all about, Red?"

"Of course, I don't really know, but my guess is that our government had some message to give to Mao Tse-tung, and we didn't want Chinag to know anything about it. The secrecy was important because Americans never made a move that the Generalissimo didn't know about. His Nationalist spies were everywhere. Someone just told me a few days ago that the Communists took the airport in Hsian. Remember all those *pings* we saw around there? They must have figured the time was ripe for picking off the airfield."

"Maybe someday you'll find out that your flight to Yenan had a big political punch to it," I teased.

After we had dinner at the club, we looked around for either a rickshaw or a taxi to take us back to the hospital. The streets were noisy, the unrest of the populace was evidenced in a subtle way, but before long it was plain to see that the whole city was being unrestrainedly torn apart. We saw the rioting people overturn a British vehicle and set it afire. A mob surrounded us and I was terrified that we would be *gheraoed*, a particularly cruel method of intimidation that these Asian people resorted to. They silently formed a circle around the victim and simply kept that person captive, no physical harm to the person but a large dose of psychological terror. We explained that we were Americans, not British. One Indian pinned a Gandhi button on my uniform which I accepted willingly, not only because I was frightened but because I believed that Mohandas Gandhi was the noble leader that the Indians needed. To have millions of people living in a muck-heap, chained to their misery by poverty and ignorance, was an affront to my American way of thinking. The moment, however, demanded a quick departure from the streets to the safety of the military hospital compound. The next day a messenger came to the BOQ where Red was staying. The USS *General Bliss* was docked at Calcutta and ready to take on its cargo of eager homebound troops. For a brief moment, as we said goodbye, the world shut down to only ourselves, but that time quickly evaporated into the stark reality that soon we would not even be living on the same side of the planet.

Chapter 19

A New Year's Eve Escapade

T HE HOLIDAY SEASON was especially painful for Americans away
from home. Christmas, in my mind, was bound up with snow and
fir trees, wintry settings, warm firesides, and traditional family dinners
that this part of the world did not provide. The men in the ward fash-
ioned a tree out of palm fronds, decorated it with handmade paper
images of Santa, bells, trees, and sleighs, hoping to elevate the holiday
spirits of all of us. It was such a watered down effort to bring gaiety
to Christmas, that it was more depressing than just leaving the whole
thing alone and allowing the date on the calendar to pass, noticed but
not magnified into something that it couldn't be. We gathered in the
wards on Christmas Eve and sang the lovely old carols that were familiar to all of us; we didn't even need the printed words for as Americans most of us shared a common knowledge of this music. Our singing
came as close to the heart of Christmas as anything we did, but the
real joy came from knowing that the flow of homebound troops was
growing every day. The USS *General Bliss* had, I supposed, arrived in
New York, and Red was spending the holidays with his family. It was
the first Christmas in many years when the violent noises of war did
not resound from somewhere on the earth.

Mitzi and I were invited by some British officers to go to Hastings Mill to a New Year's Eve party. There was an elegant club there,
established decades ago, bearing the name of the first governor general of India. We accepted their invitation and then a devilish idea
began to brew in my mind.

"Mitzi, I'm going to be a tea planter's daughter on New Year's
Eve," I giggled.

"You're going to be what?" she asked, looking at me as though I'd
lost my marbles.

"Remember that long dress in the bottom of my foot locker? Well, I think I'll wear that and forget about this shirt and tie stuff."

"Hey, wait a minute." Mitzi could not have been more alarmed if I'd told her I planned to rob a bank. "That's cause for a court-martial, you know, being out of uniform in a public place."

"The war's over, Mitzi, and there aren't many M.P.s around anymore. If anyone asks, I'm just a British girl who's been here all her life." I said this to her in my best British accent, still convinced that wearing that wonderful white gown would give me a delicious feeling of being a person again, not just another olive drab cog in the wheel.

"Well, if you're dead set on doing it, here's something to go with your outfit." She handed me a long ivory cigarette holder. "I'm going to make believe I don't know you, in case you get caught, so be sure to take off your dog tags, too."

"Dog tags with an evening dress?" I gasped.

We laughed at the thought of pulling off this little deception, which to me didn't seem like such a big deal. Just to get gussied up like a real girl, to sweep over the dance floor to the music of the orchestra, to enter a land of make-believe and blot out the reality of the present that hung around my neck like a deadly encumbrance. In retrospect, this behavior was more a symptom of adolescence than nascent adulthood—a girl putting clothing on her daydreams.

"At midnight we're going for a boat ride, up the Hooghly River," Mitzi told me.

"That'll be different. Sounds like fun. Remember watching the ball drop in Times Square, Mitzi?"

"That seems like a hundred years ago," she sighed, "but I can hear Guy Lombardo's 'Auld Lang Syne' right now."

"What's the boat like, the one we're going up river in?" I was wondering if my little conspiracy to dress like a civilian would hold up if the boat was one of those primitive vessels I had seen on the river.

"Real posh," Mitzi answered.

New Year's Eve came, the last day of 1945. The festivities at this fashionable British club were elegant. Dancing to the music that belonged to the war years, sparkling conversation of cosmopolitan company, and drinking spirits that were always a major part of every gathering, helped to make it so. I had become adroit at making one gimlet last all night, at stretching a brandy and soda over hours, for I simply could not tolerate liquor in any significant quantity. Besides, I had this dread of being out of control, of being in a state where I would perhaps do or say something that I'd regret forever. The Limey officer I was with loved having his date dressed up as much as I enjoyed the swish of jersey as we glided over the dance floor. He made me feel much more comfortable when he said that the club was not really a public place and dressing in civvies was perfectly smashing, and that I was the most beautiful American girl he knew. I dared to believe that what he whispered in my ear was true, even though his words were flattery, pure and simple. My flawless complexion had lost its jaundiced color because we were not taking atabrine—Calcutta, in the dry season, held a much reduced threat of malaria—but beyond this youthful glow there was no rare beauty. My innermost dream was always to be thin and willowy, but, as my mother described me, I was "chunky." I saw only two other Americans there, Mitzi and a Red Cross woman whom I had never met.

As midnight approached, we stepped out of the club and walked to a small pier where several boats were anchored and the four of us climbed into the boat while the Hindu oarsman pushed us out into the river. There was no escape from the odors that hung over the water, but I had become accustomed to Calcutta stench and now hoped that we would not run upon the corpse of an animal floating in the current. Along the banks, we could see a few gnats where the fires were built to cremate the dead, embers still glowing. Other small vessels were plowing the waters and in the distance the great docks were visible, docks that berthed the mighty ships that sailed round the world. All that our eyes could discern in the darkness was most uninteresting compared to the beauty of the moon and the sky. The night was soft and still, and the moonlight crept across the river in a path of golden ripples. A new year was being born, a year released from the bondage of war, a year when the fragments of our lives would coalesce into the mosaic of our individual selves. My date said he would much rather be paddling up the Thames, but even that could not possibly have been as lovely as the Hooghly was this night.

We left Hastings Mill at around two o'clock in the morning. The moon, now far above the horizon, floated like a pearl in the fathomless sky, a reminder that war and all human upheavals have no impact whatsoever in the larger scheme of things. On the way home, Mitzi suggested that we stop at the British American Club and round out the night with another drink to celebrate the New Year. Many of our American friends were certain to be there and we wished to share a New Year *chotapeg* with them. Everyone was agreeable, so, filled with good cheer, we elbowed our way into the overcrowded club and looked for a table where we could sit. Someone beckoned to Mitzi. I turned, only to come face to face with our chief nurse, who, though quite under the influence of a night of drinking, was still not too sauced to see that I was out of uniform. Her tie was askew, her coat half off, and she was clearly drowning whatever sorrows she had in gin and squash. It seemed odd that she made no comment about my being out of uniform, perhaps in exchange for my overlooking her state of drunkenness, I thought. Leaving that place was uppermost in my mind for my holiday spirits were sinking faster than a stone in a mill-pond, and I was uneasy every minute I sat there.

"Mitzi, I'm in big trouble," I whispered.

"You bet you are." This comment didn't do much to ease my discomfort. "I'll urge the guys to take us home as soon as possible. What a way to begin a new year!" Mitzi was really fed up with my little theatrical prank, I could tell, even though it was no skin off her nose.

The next day while I was working on the ward, just as I expected, a message came for me to report to the major. I truly had to jack up my courage to walk into her office with any degree of composure. One look at the expression on her face, and I knew I'd be spending the rest of my life in Leavenworth. I saluted smartly.

"At ease, Lieutenant," she said, but she didn't look me in the eye. "Being out of uniform is behavior unbecoming to an officer," she continued, "therefore, you are confined to the hospital compound for a week. Dismissed."

I was never so glad to leave a place as I was to walk out of that office. "Behavior unbecoming an officer?" How about the condition she was in; was that becoming to an officer? Hardly. That was not even becoming to a lady. I felt myself fortunate to have gotten off with the mild punishment she had doled out to me, and I had no intention of doing anything more than accepting it and abiding by it. She outranked me, significantly. She was a major and I was the lowest officer on the totem pole, a mere shavetail, a second lieutenant.

There wasn't much pain in having to stay in the compound for a week, the agony came whenever anyone I knew gave me that sidelong glance that made me feel like a criminal of sorts. One night was taken up with a USO show at Monsoon Square Gardens, within the compound, other evenings I spent writing letters and getting my gear in condition in the event that new orders came through. It was safer to be in our own area than elsewhere, as the city was becoming increasingly dangerous with the rioting that preceded the coming elections. Even the British were evacuating troops from the urban regions. Time seemed to be halted in this early part of the year. I was still assigned to care for the tragic young man who was showing little if any improvement in his recovery from polio. We practiced our best isolation techniques in our nursing care of this patient as a respiratory infection would have been a lethal development. As soon as all his physical needs were met, I read to him. This brought great pleasure for only then did I ever see him smile. At the end of each day, I had Lily serve tea on the long ramp where I sat in that world of daydreams that had overtaken my life.

Chapter 20

Left Behind in India

COMING OFF DUTY one day, I heard female voices blended in boisterous hilarity. Our barracks had broken out with so much happiness that it was hard to equate that much joy with a single piece of paper that was being passed around. Printed on the paper were orders for almost everyone in the barracks as well as the rest of the compound. Many of the girls were returning to the ZI, among them, Mitzi.

"I can't believe this is happening. Someone said there's a liberty ship in the harbor, and they're hoping to fill it up. Wow, this is the best news I've seen in months." Mitzi was wild with the thought of home, as were many of the other nurses.

"Am I on the list?" I was stretching and straining to see the paper that she held.

"You're not listed on this sheet," Mitzi said, "but there could be other orders posted in the mess." She was trying to make me feel good, but I intuitively knew that for the first time, she and I did not have the same orders. She was going home and I was stuck; it was as plain as that. I felt a lump form in my throat, a balling up of tears that would burst through if I tried to talk, so I just watched as everyone else's exhilaration flooded the barracks. It was the same feeling I had experienced when everyone in the first grade was promoted to second grade and I, because whooping cough had kept me from going to school the better part of the year, was the only one remaining. That same feeling of having been forsaken by everyone swept over me, as it had done when I was five years old. How could I possibly survive in the Army without Mitzi? She had been the one person I could lean on, the one nurse who was willing to put up with my immaturity and help me to understand the ways of the world. Later, I learned that there were others whose names were not on the list, a handful of us

still expected to carry on nursing service as the hospital unit continued to shrink.

Ever hoping that the rest of us would soon be leaving, I went to
our chief nurse and requested air transportation home. It seemed possible that if we could fly home we'd get there before the ship did. My
orders soon came through, and to my dismay, I was assigned to the 181st
General Hospital in Karachi. I, together with a few other nurses,
packed my gear and prepared for yet another long stretch of time before
going home. No mail was getting to us, probably because the units
were in such a state of transition. Climbing aboard the transport
brought memories of Kismet as we settled into the old bucket seats
and the friendly drone of the plane carried us high into the clear dome
of blue that hangs over India before the onset of another monsoon season. The pilot took us to Agra where we visited the Taj Mahal. Like
a jewel, that magnificent mausoleum sits on the flat plain of the Jumna,
a tributary of the Ganges, and seems to play with the lights reflecting
from the red sandstone earth. Pale pinks and lavenders shimmer up and
down its white marble walls. To see such beauty in a land where I had
seen the ugliness of poverty and disease, reminded me again of the
incredible diversity of this nation. One can no more say that New York
is what the United States is all about, than one can say Calcutta or
Assam is a representation of India. From the frosted Himalayas, to the
burning desert sands, to the tropical forests, to the straw hut villages,
to the great metropolis of Calcutta—it is all India, with endless vari-
ations. I was on the threshold of seeing another part of this extraordinary country that defies description.

Our flight arrived after the fall of darkness in Karachi, and we
were transported to an army base in a weapons carrier. This was the
desert, cold and clear, silent under a star-studded sky, where the view
of the rolling land was broken only with the silhouettes of small villages, of mosques and their minarets. Before the truck pulled up to the
place where we would be billeted, I reached down to my side where I
had placed the zippered briefcase that I took wherever I went. Inside
was my 201 file, my records of personal information and military activity, and an accumulation of letters, notes, photographs—all my papers
which affirmed my identity.

"Hold everything!" I shouted to the other people on the truck.
"I've lost my briefcase. Look around on the floor, please." A thorough

search of the vehicle produced nothing. I knew that either it had slid off the truck or a thieving hand had found its way under the tarp of the truck and snatched it away. I felt disoriented without this briefcase and its contents, for it had been with me from my inception into the Army until this moment when the end of my tour of duty was almost in sight. Somewhere in my deepest understanding of things, I knew that had Mitzi been here my briefcase would never have vanished while my attention was distracted. It was a shattering loss. The contents could not be replaced. There were addresses of people I had met, there were some priceless photographs, there were accurate records of places where I had been assigned.

Again we were deposited in a barracks. After putting our gear away, several of us found the Officers' Club. The first person I ran into there was Tex. He had been assigned to the medical staff at the 181st but was leaving the next day for Kanchapara where he would stay to provide medical services to the troops until the whole theater was evacuated. We had a wonderful evening rehashing those months of misery in the monsoon wetness of Assam.

"Hey, what ever happened to the 'fly boy' who stole you away from me?" Tex asked.

"Well, he was in China for a while. He stopped to see me when he came back to Calcutta on his way home. He left on the Bliss and expected to be home for Christmas."

"You in love with him?" Tex asked. I could feel his eyes riveted on my face, looking for my reaction to his question.

"I don't know," I lied. "How do you know when you love someone, especially when that person is far away? It's easy to fall in love with your own imaginings, I suppose."

"I wish I wasn't leaving tomorrow," he said, and he wrapped his arms around me and held me until I broke the silence.

"What's going on at the 181st?" I asked.

"It's closing. That's why I'm going to Kanchapara," he told me.

"That means we won't be going on duty."

There were ten of us, and we had come all across India, only to find out that when the USS *General Morton* arrived in Karachi we would board her and sail back to the States. Air transportation was simply unavailable to nurses. In the meantime, we could spend our hours in any way we liked.

Karachi, like Calcutta, had been a port for the reception of troops and matériel into the CBI. It was used extensively during the time that Japan's prowling submarines controlled the Pacific, for at that time all shipping was unsafe in those enemy waters. The base, Camp Malir, where we were quartered was some distance from the hospital and as it turned out we never saw the inside of the 181st. As military installations go, it was enormous. Here was the place where the British had trained their troops in desert warfare, the Desert Rats who fought against Rommel in the north of Africa. Row upon row of barracks sat hollow on the sand; the ghosts of war hovered over the land.

It was from Camp Malir that we made our final exit from the CBI. No one knew, or no one informed any of us when the ship was due in the port of Karachi, so, as we had done many times before, we kept our gear in readiness and tried to shorten the creeping hours with useful exploration and relaxing camaraderie. The impatience of youth was getting a severe testing. We felt like stragglers on a long journey to freedom. Most of our thinking was directed not to the upcoming trip but to the final destination. We had begun to think of America as a veritable utopia, remembering in a distorted way what things were like back home. The family farm in Pennsylvania was a haven of abundance; I had forgotten what a stingy living the rock-strewn fields yielded. The towns and villages were neat, with clean streets of modest homes; I had forgotten how shabby the clapboard houses became while the men were off to war. The hospital where I had been schooled was a bustling complex of professionals dedicated to healing; I had forgotten the long hours of drudgery and the caste system that held the nurse servile to the physician. The dreams that we conjured up far outstretched reality, but brought infinite comfort to us in our eagerness to leave India and get on with life.

In the meantime, we wanted to become familiar with this part of India, which was so unlike the province of Assam or the great metropolis of Calcutta. Karachi, though it smelled of camel dung, did not have those nauseating odors that marked so many Oriental cities, nor did it have an uncomfortable climate at this time of the year. The absence of humidity was delightful after being soaked in the vapors of eastern India. The buildings, painted in pleasing pastels, stretched far into the nearby desert. We walked the board avenues and peeked into the narrow alleys and the bustling bazaars. Where we had once seen Hindu

Riding camels on shore of Arabian Sea near Karachi. We were just waiting to go home and filled our idle hours with play. (Author on left.)

women with the vermilion *tikka* on their foreheads, we now saw Moslem women hidden beneath their black veils. The men wore voluminous trousers instead of the *dhoti*. The language on the streets was now Urdu instead of the more familiar Hindi. From the mosques, a *muezzin* called the faithful Moslems to worship; the sound, a shrill command that broke through the clear, dry desert air bending the citizens until their faces touched the holy ground. Unaware of it at the time, memories were being permanently etched on my young brain, the picture of row upon row of bowed heads in and around the mosque was one of them.

One day, a few of the nurses and some of the other officers waiting for the ship got a jeep from the motor pool and headed for the ocean. The coastline was a great unbroken expanse, except for the mouths of the Indus, where the Thar Desert sweeps down to the sea. The brown land met the violet colored water in an unruffled, silent, resplendent beauty. We met a man with a camel walking on the beach. We asked for a ride, and quite to our surprise, he commanded the beast to kneel. We sat upon the beast's bony convexity and rode to the water's edge. Our trousers picked up the filth that was encrusted on the animal's back, so we decided to rid ourselves of the dirt by going into the inviting water. The wetness felt good on our legs and thighs and we romped about until our play disintegrated into a merciless splashing of each other. The air dried us off quickly and the sea water was refreshing after the dry heat of the afternoon sun. The man with the camel waited patiently until we handed him a few rupees, then led his haughty charge down the beach toward a caravan that was resting by the sea.

Chapter 21

Going Home

THE USS *GENERAL MORTON* finally arrived in the port of Karachi, gathered up its cargo of impatient men and women and set sail for America. Among the passengers were a few war brides and several small children. One GI had married a Burmese girl who had a two year old son. They shared a stateroom with us. When the PA system announced that there was water for showers, we all rushed to bathe, but the Burmese woman would not remove her clothing. She showered with all her garments on, then went out on deck and let the breeze do the drying.

Food served in the officers' mess was the first thing that made us feel the reality of home. Fresh butter replaced the "vaseline" that came to us in olive drab cans; ice-cream, something we had never seen in India, was served every day; fresh meat appeared on the table and tasted delicious after months of eating Spam, but there were no fresh or raw vegetables served, and that is what we hungered for the most.

"I can't believe we're finally on our way," I said to one of the other nurses as we leaned on the rail and watched the land fade into the horizon.

"I can't get excited about it," she answered, "but that's because it doesn't seem real to me, either."

"Everyone aboard acts as though they're headed for the gallows. Did you ever see such a gloomy bunch? The troops coming over were so loud and filled with spirit. We had a band on board, music every day, and an enthusiasm that isn't here now."

"Maybe the climate left everyone tired and washed-out," she suggested.

That seemed too simple a solution to me. I felt that what I'd done for the war effort was insignificant, that I'd been shuffled from one place to another and wasted precious time, that I'd had to adjust to short periods of hard work, short periods of absolutely nothing to do, and long periods poised to react to some order that had been issued by someone who had no knowledge of what was really going on. I had once harbored the thought of staying in the military, but thought better of it when I realized how frustrating it was to be so manipulated. Now, thinking about how subdued everyone was, I attributed some of it to the helplessness that an individual feels when his every move is controlled by an enormous, impersonal organization like the Army. And those of us who had gone to war with visions of glory in our innocent heads, had learned that war is a weary process, fought in short bursts on the battlefield and in long, exhausting hours of attrition. Our experience in the CBI had disillusioned us when we became aware of the perfidy that our allies practiced in that campaign. Returning from the war in Asia did not carry the same robust expressions of approval as from the European theater.

We sailed through the Arabian Sea, down the Malabar Coast and laid anchor at the port of Colombo on the island of Ceylon, now Sri Lanka. Here I was able to post letters home so my family could follow the ship arrivals and know when we were at last on our own shores. We sailed across the Indian Ocean, through the Strait of Malacca that lies between Sumatra and Malaya, stopped briefly in Singapore, then on into the South China Sea. The scuttlebutt was that the skipper of our ship was going to retire after this voyage and he was stopping off at a number of places to say farewell to his old Navy friends. The ship headed for Manila where the passengers would be allowed a few days shore leave.

It was a glorious morning when we slid through the narrow channel of water that separates the Bataan Peninsula from the rock that is Corregidor. We stood on the deck, eyes glued to the small white crosses that marched up the hillside. They seemed close enough to reach out and touch. There was an awful finality in their dazzling whiteness and their cold silence, a piercing reminder of the brave men and women who had tried so hard to keep the Philippines from falling to the enemy.

If ever the American nurses had distinguished themselves, it was here. They had evacuated Bataan and set up a hospital in the rock tunnel on Corregidor, ministering to the thousands of battle casualties, while bombs exploded overhead and all around them. But Corregidor fell to the Japanese and many of the nurses were taken prisoner (the official number is 67 Army nurses and 11 Navy nurses). Some of them spent three years interned by the enemy, and some of these white crosses were placed there for other nurses who died in the conflict. I wondered as the ship sailed on into Manila Bay if the world would ever recognize women's contribution to the war effort. Could a woman ever be thought of as a hero?

As we approached Manila, we saw the palm trees standing at half mast, as artillery fire had cut every tree to half its original height. Even though we Americans were victors, it seemed inappropriate to rejoice, for an inexplicable sadness permeated everything related to the war. We sailed away from Manila and into Subic Bay.

While the ship's captain went about his business, he offered shore leave to the officers who were passengers. We visited a town called Olongapo, a wild village that seemed to exist mostly for our own sailors. It was a town of drinking, gambling, prostitution—truly a den of iniquity. It was a relief to get away from such an environment and head out to sea again. We stopped at Eniwetok in the Marshall Islands, a brown pancake floating on a brilliant blue sea, where only a few quonset huts and fewer palm trees broke the unending horizon. Here we gathered up more Navy personnel to bring home. The ship was filled to the gunwales with men and women who had been away a very long time. The captain announced that there would be no more delays, that the USS *General Morton* was on its way to San Francisco, and he wished us a pleasant voyage.

There was a great feeling of expectancy among us, the certainty that just getting home would be the answer to every dilemma that we had ever faced.

"This is taking forever," I commented to one of the ship's officers. "It's like being in a row boat with only one oar."

"You've forgotten how wide the Pacific is. Enjoy it," was his laconic answer.

I sat on the deck and drank in the vastness of sea and sky and tried to fabricate a future for myself. There was a time when I really had felt like a nurse, confident in my ability to promote healing and wellness in the sick. The aura of assurance that had enveloped my starchy whiteness was replaced with a bedraggled khaki insecurity about my own abilities. After nursing in a muddy, thatched roof hospital

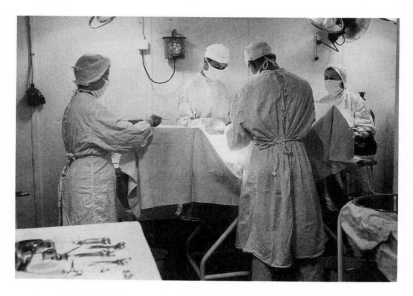

Scrubbed for minor surgery on board ship during return voyage.

where techniques were modified beyond recognition, would I be able to function in a modern aseptic setting? While I reflected on the decadence of my nursing arts, a ship's officer came to the nurses' area and asked for a volunteer to assist with a minor surgery in sick bay. I was delighted to help with the incision and drainage of an axillary abscess and when the work was completed I realized how much I missed being useful and busy.

I thought about Red and wondered what it would be like to see him again. It was not possible to visualize him in any other roll than the nonchalant lieutenant I had known in Ledo, nor in any other place but those where we had been together: the airbase's Officers' Club, the *basha* at the 14th Evac., the cockpit of Kismet, the streets of Calcutta, Chungking, and Hsian. We had been separated for months and I was quite unable to know whether or not I was still in love. That curious fascination with the opposite sex seemed to be a primary ingredient of life, an innate force that propelled my thinking to marriage and all that it implied. Being in love, for me, at that time in my life, meant getting married, having babies and nesting with someone who would always be there to take care of me. For my generation of young women, that was the ultimate goal. Having a professional career was an option just beginning to come into vogue, so I sometimes surreptitiously entertained the idea of continuing my education and finding a niche outside the confines of matrimony. At twenty-two, I hadn't the faintest inkling that life was finite; the fantasy of immortality offered a plethora of possibilities.

One morning a voice from the PA system fractured the quiet on the ship. "Land ahoy!" In less time than I thought possible, the decks were swarming. Everyone was straining to get a view of something besides blue water, but I failed to see anything beyond the frothy swells that opened pleasantly to let the big liberty ship grind forward.

"We will be sailing under the Golden Gate Bridge and into San Francisco Bay before noon." These words coming over the PA system were a signal for the loudest explosion of screaming and yelling that I had ever experienced anywhere. The USS *General Morton*, with its cargo of yelping warriors, was at last nearing the inviolable shores of America. Tears, laughter, embraces and shouts of joy sent everyone's dignity over the side. Euphoria reigned. As we slipped under the bridge, a small boat came out to meet us. On the deck was a military band thumping out all the soul-stirring music ever written, and mellowing down into "God Bless America." I wept unashamedly.

Patriotism is an emotion difficult to define. It is all the Gilbert Stuart portraits of George Washington in every school room in America. It is not only the "Star Spangled Banner," but also the sounds of big band music. It is the sight of farmers in bib overalls who stand at the edge of the cornfields and watch the automobiles rattle over country roads. It is FDR's rakish smile and Eisenhower's boyish grin. It is the stars and stripes flapping high over the capitol dome. It is a personal relationship with my own country, and as a child feels that his parents are perfect and omniscient, so I felt was the nation that we called America.

There was a lot of sorting out to be done before each of us was assigned transportation home. For some, there was a short bus ride to the Presidio, for others trains to Texas and trains to Seattle, but for many of us it would be a four day ride by rail over the breadth of the nation. Calling home was first on everyone's list so the queues at the telephones were long and tedious.

"Mom! I'm home!" I wondered if hearing those words was as exhilarating as speaking them. And then, as the conversation continued
there was the feeling of never having been away. All those months were
ripped off the calendar, but the calendar was still there with a picture
of April's tulips bending in the spring breeze. I guess I expected enormous changes in everything, but sameness pervaded life back home,
the same mundane concerns that had always been there. I thought I
should telephone Red but my courage failed. What would he be doing
if he wasn't flying a plane? What would we talk about? How would he
like my humble, rustic parents? Suddenly I wished that I had never
met him, that he had never waggled his wings at me, that we had never
slipped off into China and soared in the skies over the Himalayas.
Coming home was not all gladness and cheer; I felt sad and dispirited,
a walking toy winding down to prosaic reality.

The *San Francisco Overland* was much more comfortable than the
train that carried us to our POE. In the dining cars, we were served
crisp green salads that disappeared as quickly as the scenery in the
windows. Gradually we were warming to the thought of home; the
great expanses of open country gave us the feel of America, and wherever we stopped and left the train, the people greeted us as though we
were heroes. Coming from the war in Asia, they knew we had "licked
the Japs," and that was all that mattered to the ordinary citizen.

When the train stopped in Chicago, I had mustered enough
courage to telephone Red. He sounded like a little kid on the phone.
I realized that we had never communicated over the Bell system, that
our serious dialogue had been a dipping of wings, a wave and a roaring away over the treetops.

"I'll be in Fort Dix on Tuesday," I told him.

"Are you being mustered out?" he asked.

"Yes, I am, Red."

"Could you call me Art? No one calls me Red. That was over
there. This is different."

But it wasn't different. When I saw him, when he reached out for
me and I heard his soft voice, when I saw the melting look of love in
his eyes, I felt the same fever that I had known back in Ledo, and knew
there was no recovery from such an affliction.

Epilogue

W E HAD RETURNED to an America that was still exhaling the sigh of relief that the war was history, but moving onward with such swiftness and vigor that no one thought about resting on triumphal laurels. Those of us who had been away really didn't want to talk about it and those who stayed home didn't seem very interested. We were truly a one-directional society: forward. It looked as though we were making a clean break with the past. With scarcely a backward glance, everyone sought a position in the mainstream of things, hoping to grow in all directions: economically, educationally, professionally and industrially.

There were shortages of goods even more acute than when the war was at its peak. There were no nylon stockings because nylon had been used to make parachutes. Bed sheets were impossible to find because the textile industry had been turning out canvas for tents, uniforms, and every kind of cotton goods needed by the military. Food products were in short supply and would continue to be while we sent our agricultural products aboard to the starving European nations. However, rationing of some food items lasted for only a few months, whereas rationing continued in England for more than five years. Imported things like tea, coffee, and spices were not easily available until the shipping industry recovered. The automobile manufacturers had to make the big changeover from tank and truck production to the family car, a high priority item on everyone's want list. And that segment of manufacturing was to become the engine that pulled the entire economy into a new era of national prosperity. Housing was scarce; returning veterans could not find suitable places to live. Then houses began coming onto the market in a way that was new to America— each little home was exactly like the others in a row upon row of what we called "ticky-tacky" communities. I never was discomfited by these deficiencies because I felt that the old work ethic was alive and well, that eventually all good things would be available to us. Remarkably, the economy was able to make the transition to peacetime without ruinous inflation and without price controls.

We packed away our uniforms along with our memories and began the hot pursuit of the American dream. The GI Bill of Rights, offering the opportunity for education was one of the wisest and most appreciated pieces of legislation that ever came out of Washington. Art and I both enrolled in school and while we waited for the semester to begin we found jobs.

It was not possible to just pick up where we had left off, as was sometime expected of us, because we had changed. I took a position as a staff nurse in a reputable hospital, but on my first day on duty the head nurse asked me to clean beds and windowsills in the ward, work that housekeeping services should have been doing. When I reached for a patient's chart to study his medical record, she asked me to wait until she had time to explain the diagnosis to me. I was appalled. Having had a position of leadership in the military, this irked me, but my Army-born respect for authority was still in place, so I did what I was asked to do. It became clear that my professional colleagues who had remained in civilian positions had little appreciation for the liberating effect the war had on those of us who served our country. Doubtless, many civilian nurses had worked under difficult conditions as a result of shortages of personnel and their sacrifices were not to be undervalued. Although we may have suffered a multiplicity of miseries in our wartime assignments, there had also been times when life had been a lark. There were no particular expressions of appreciation for service to our country and I cannot recall having expected any. Women in the service were still an aberration.

It was while working in this hospital in Glen Ridge, New Jersey, that I met the father of the RAF officer who had greeted us at Alipore Airport near Calcutta. He was a patient who had a private duty nurse caring for him. She wanted to be off for a day so I agreed to "special" her patient. When I told him I had just returned from overseas he said, "I have a son in India who has been gone for seven years. He was working for an oil company and when war broke out he joined the RAF and has been on active duty since then." It was an incredible coincidence that I had seen his son just a few months ago and was able to convey the fact of his well-being to his father.

The romance that had begun with a waggle of wings in a far off place took root on native soil and flourished. Art and I were married before the year ended. There was one poignant moment at our wedding when the whole Asian experience burst into the present—the thundering voice of a baritone soloist singing "On the Road to Mandalay." In my mind's eye, there flashed images of us together in our old wrinkled khakis soaring over the snow-covered peaks, dancing at that Officers' Club in Ledo, eating in the shack on stilts that we dared to call a restaurant. But the present was too much with us; we rarely, if ever, talked about the embryonic stages of our love for each other.

In 1987, we returned to China. We drove through the same gate in the wall around Xian that we had driven through in 1945 while the Communist soldiers waited outside to capture the airfield. Riding in a tourists' bus didn't hold a candle to roaring through in a jeep, with the heart under my caduceus beating in rhythm to the heart under his wings.

In the center of the city, the Chinese had built a beautiful hotel, the Golden Flower, much like western hotels, meant to promote an atmosphere of affluence. We were not fooled. Even from the window of our hotel room, the old China that we had known kept surfacing: the single water faucet that served dozens of families in their cramped little brick and mortar houses; the queue of men and women waiting to rinse their rice bowls, fill their basins, and wash their sun-baked faces; the bicycle carrying a burden equal to what a pick-up truck could manage. However, Xian's food markets were filled with produce, foot-long string beans, egg plants, all kinds of "green-leafies" and heaps of watermelons. It was comforting to know that the populace was eating well. The faces of the children were radiant, unlike those sad little figures that I remembered seeing back in 1945. And again I heard that musical laughter, that spontaneous eruption of amusement that I shall always identify with these patient, long-suffering people.

The magnificent terra cotta warriors that had stood undisturbed in their ancient grave while China wrestled with yet another enemy, had been unearthed and were now on display. They are an awesome sight. We were reminded of China's long history, and cognizant of the trivial role our nation played in it. All our efforts in behalf of Chiang

Kai-shek and his Nationalist armies were like writing on water. When we saw all the monuments in Taiwan erected to the glory of this man, we remarked to each other that "in the end he was little more than an old-fashioned Chinese *tuchun* (warlord)."

In Shanghai, we stayed at another of those western style hotels. From the balcony of our room, we looked out over a city that cowered under a canopy of filthy brown smog. As far as the eye could see, the neglected buildings spread from the Bund, north and westward toward the mighty Yangtze River, a decaying monument to a form of government blind to the aesthetic dimensions of urban life. All the new buildings were utilitarian structures of gray concrete, bearing no mark of tradition or artistic form, but creating a monotonous ugliness on the landscape. The one thing that seemed truly Chinese to me was the bamboo scaffolding at all these construction sites. It was temporary, of course, but more graceful than the permanent buildings behind its myriad squares. We went to the Sun Ya restaurant on Nanking Road, surprised that it still existed and that it bore the same name. What once had been a luxurious place to dine was now a dirty, run-down dive where soiled tablecloths were set with cracked and chipped dishes, where the odor of overheated grease permeated the air. Children, unattended by parents, ran under and around tables. Art was crestfallen when he remembered the ten-course dinner that had been so elegantly served here, the dignified Oriental atmosphere, and the graciousness of his two Chinese hosts.

Very soon after I left Calcutta in 1946, the violence between Hindus and Muslims exploded into the bloody massacre that presaged the partition of India, creating a divided Pakistan. These events marked the beginning of the end for Calcutta. A huge Hindu refugee population moved into the city, expanded all the outlying areas into unspeakable slums, and initiated the decay of a once mighty metropolis. Now the dirty brown exhaust from buses and cars hangs over the squalor. The roads are in disrepair and fissured with open drainage ditches. When the monsoon rains come, the city is waterlogged for days on end. Dead animals are not immediately removed from the streets, so it is not unusual to see the bloated carcass of a cow lying in the accumulation of water. I am glad that I experienced Calcutta when the British influence was still so apparent for I cannot imagine the poverty being greater than it was when I was there.

After I had completed writing this book, I learned more about the plane crash that had taken the lives of eighteen nurses. A woman who now lives in Maine and watches for fires in the forestlands near the coast had served as a nurse in the CBI and was there when this tragedy happened. She remembered the details clearly and told me about the nurse who had committed suicide because she was so overcome with grief at the loss of her many friends.

The Air Commandos, of which Art's squadron was a part, had a reunion, where, for the first time in forty-five years he met with the men who had flown with him in the conflict that had carried them to the distant borders of China, Burma and India. I went too. Where I had once seen the clear, cool virility of young men, I looked upon a sea of graying heads and seamed faces. The men were seduced by memories of themselves as gallant fliers, but whatever pleasure they derived from this seduction, they deserved it. Some of the men had gone on to seek professions, some to build businesses, others to take over farms that had always been in their families. One of the men from the squadron had become the general manager of the Metropolitan Opera Company, a reminder of the diversity that existed in the men who had gone to war. Each, in his unique way, had, as we had done, made a contribution to his country.

Our children seem to think of World War II as a fairy tale, perhaps because of the great advances that have been made since then. Aircraft built today can soar over those towering mountains with little effort and no fear of being unable to reach high altitudes. Scarcely a place on earth is remote anymore, and what was once far away is now measured by the several hours that it takes to get there. Sometimes I think of how different nursing would have been in our thatched roof hospital if we had had the powerful infection fighting drugs that are here today.

Art's hair is no longer red, but white as the snows that blanket many of those lonely Himalayan peaks that stab at the doors of heaven. I am no longer the radiant girl who dared to climb into Kismet and skim the heights of uncharted mountains. We have lived long and happily together, holding in our hearts a deathless memory.

Index

Air Transport Command 11, 92
Aircraft: AT-9 78; B-25 144; C-47
   7, 54, 61, 70, 72, 94, 103, 110, 127
Alipore, India 74
Assam, India 7, 11, 15, 22, 23, 24,
   42, 76, 78, 81, 97, 104, 105, 117,
   122, 128, 130, 159
Atabrine 16, 79, 105
Australia 34, 35, 119

Bataan (Philippines) 164
Bay of Bengal 36, 67, 88
Beale, Camp 30, 126
Brahmaputra River 73, 88
British American Club 137, 138,
   149, 150, 155
Burma Road 7

Calcutta, India 11, 16, 22, 34, 36,
   61, 70, 71, 72, 73, 74, 75, 78, 80,
   81, 83, 90, 94, 105, 119, 123, 128,
   130, 131, 137, 141, 143, 154, 166
Chabua, India 11, 12, 62, 91, 92
Chiang Kai-shek 8, 56, 89, 95, 100,
   111, 115, 117, 128, 130, 145, 150, 171
Chowringhee Road 75, 141
Christmas 144, 152
Chungking, China 90, 91, 92, 95,
   96, 97, 99, 100, 101, 115, 117, 130,
   166
Chunglung Po Airport 97, 117

Communists 52, 56, 95, 96, 111,
   113, 115, 116, 117, 128, 129, 141, 144

Dum Dum Airport 74, 142
Dysentery 43, 44, 45, 46, 59, 66, 79

Eniwetok (Marshall Islands) 165

Firpo's 137, 141, 149
Fort Dix 26, 27, 168

Gandhi, Mohandas 141, 151
Ganges River 36, 73, 158
Great Wall 116, 144
Gurkhas 62, 66, 67, 78
Gymkhana Club 137

Hooghly River 36, 74, 77, 153, 154
Hospitals: 14th Evacuation 8, 12,
   19, 22, 39, 41, 42, 43, 46, 57, 64,
   65, 81, 88, 89, 92, 93, 104, 105,
   109, 111, 117, 125, 132, 166; 20th
   General 11, 42, 80, 120, 121, 123,
   125, 127; 142nd General 37, 75,
   76, 121, 127, 131, 133; 181st General 160
Hsian, China 113, 115, 116, 117, 144,
   150, 151, 166
Imphal, India 61, 62

Imphal, India 61, 62
Irrawaddy River 65, 68, 94, 101, 103

Kalaikunda, India 67, 78
Karachi, India 61, 123, 158, 159, 160
Kismet (plane) 7, 48, 58, 68, 73, 77, 89, 91
Kohima, India 61
Kunming, China 21, 56, 84, 94, 95, 96, 103, 115, 130, 143
Kuomintang 89, 96, 115, 145

Ledo, India 7, 8, 11, 12, 21, 22, 45, 50, 61, 91, 92, 93, 95, 96, 101, 103, 117, 125, 127, 166, 168
Ledo Road 7, 11, 17, 56, 71, 77, 81, 108, 113, 118, 121, 122, 145
Liangshan, China 89, 92, 101, 104, 112, 117, 125, 135, 137, 144

Malaria 16, 18, 22, 43, 46, 79, 127, 134
Mao Tse-tung 128, 144, 151
Meiktila, Burma 101
Merrill, Col. Frank 43, 121
Merrill's Marauders 43, 65
Moses Taylor Hospital 25, 123, 133
Mountbatten, Vice-Admiral Lord Louis 121
Myitkyina, Burma 21, 44, 58, 62, 65, 66, 68, 80, 88, 98

Naga Hills, India 88
Nationalists 52, 56
NY Hospital–Cornell 25, 29, 59, 133

Office of Strategic Services (OSS) 5, 8, 65, 72, 102, 105, 144
Okinawa, Japan 102

Pangsau Pass 50, 54, 56, 110
Patkai Range, India 73, 88, 93
Peking, China 147, 148
Perth, Australia 35, 119
Pick, Gen. Lewis A. 7

Ramgarh, India 39, 56
Rangoon River 66, 67, 102
Ravdin, Colonel Isidor 121
Red Cross 11, 26, 32, 91, 98, 154

Saigon, Vietnam 148
Seagrave, Dr. 62, 63, 65, 66, 71, 73, 80, 84
Shanghai, China 144, 145, 146
Shingbwiyang, Burma 12, 122
Stilwell, Gen. 8, 39, 62, 65, 66, 121, 122, 145
Stilwell Road 8, 84

Thai Air Force 143
Tinsukia, India 12, 81, 83, 88, 96
Troop Carrier 61, 67, 101, 129
Typhus 46, 79, 121

University of Pennsylvania 42, 121
USS *Gen. Bliss* 151, 152
USS *Gen. Freeman* 31, 34, 35, 36, 74, 80
USS *Gen. Morton* 159, 163, 165

Yenan, China 52, 128, 144
Yunnan Province, China 94